YOUNG STUDENTS
Learning Library®

VOLUME 17

Petroleum—
Publishing

NEWFIELD
PUBLICATIONS
SHELTON, CONNECTICUT

CREDITS

Young Students Learning Library and Newfield Publications are federally registered trademarks of Newfield Publications, Inc.

Copyright © 1995 by Newfield Publications, Inc.; 1974, 1972 by Funk & Wagnalls, Inc. & Newfield Publications, Inc.

Maps containing the appropriate Donnelley indication are copyright © 1994 by R.R. Donnelley and Sons Company. This product contains proprietary property of R.R. Donnelley & Sons Company.

Printed in the U. S. A.

ISBN 0-8374-9824-4

CONTENTS

▲ **Mount Vesuvius erupted in** A.D. **79 blanketing POMPEII with ashes.**

⚙ PETROLEUM

Petroleum is a thick liquid mostly found beneath the Earth's surface. The word *petroleum* means "rock oil." Petroleum is usually called *oil*. It ranges in color from light brown to nearly black. Most scientists believe that petroleum is the decayed remains of tiny animals and plants that lived in shallow seas millions of years ago. Heat and pressure in the Earth's crust formed layers of rock over the decaying plant and animal remains. Squeezed together, these remains turned to liquid petroleum. In this way, underground stores of petroleum were formed. Some of this petroleum was forced to the Earth's surface when the rock above it was worn down by erosion, and then cracked.

Finding Oil

People have been obtaining oil from surface pools for thousands of years. But underground petroleum was not used until 1859, when the first *oil well* (a hole drilled from the Earth's surface to an underground pool) was made by Edwin L. Drake near Titusville, Pennsylvania. His discovery, plus the invention of the internal combustion engine (which burned oil) in the late 1800s, started an oil boom that was the beginning of the petroleum industry.

The leading producers of unrefined oil are the United States and Saudi Arabia. Other major oil-producing nations include Iran, Iraq, Kuwait, Mexico, Libya, Venezuela, China, Nigeria, the United Kingdom, Indonesia, Algeria, and Canada.

Oil companies hire *geologists* to find regions where oil will most likely be found. Oil geologists explore an area by using electronic instruments that reveal what is beneath the Earth's surface. But drilling an oil well is the only way to find out for certain whether oil is located in the area. Since World War II, drilling

below the ocean floor off the coast, called *offshore drilling*, has proved very productive. Offshore oil drilling in the United States is done off the coasts of California, Texas, Louisiana, and Alaska. There are other offshore oil fields in Europe, in the North Sea, and also in Australia.

Transporting Oil

The transportation of petroleum is an important business, especially in the North Sea and in Australia. Oil is pumped from the wells through huge underground pipes, often over thousands of miles, to *refineries*. There, the crude oil is refined, or purified, and petroleum products are made. If the petroleum is not sent by pipeline, it is carried in ships called *tankers* or in railroad tank cars. The refineries deliver petroleum products using the same methods.

At an oil refinery, the various oils

▲ To reach oil layers underground, engineers drill through the rock layers. When they strike oil, it either gushes out or has to be pumped to the surface. The oil is then purified, or refined, and used to make various products, such as plastics, gasoline, and detergents.

◄ An Alaskan pipeline transporting oil to other parts of the country. Oil is Alaska's most valuable mineral product. The Arctic Coastal Plain of Alaska has large reserves of oil and natural gas.

and other materials, called *fractions*, in *crude* (unrefined) oil are separated. In the process used, called *fractional distillation*, petroleum is heated in closed containers. As the temperature

▶ Crude oil is refined to be converted into fuels and other substances that are used to make petrochemical products. The refining process involves heating the crude oil in a tower. Different *fractions,* or products, condense at different levels—the heaviest (tars) at the bottom, and the lightest (petrol) at the top.

Petroleum gases

Gasoline

Kerosene

Diesel oils

Lubricating oils

Fuel oils

Crude oil

Bitumen, asphalt, tars

is raised, one fraction after another boils. The *vapors* (gases produced by boiling) of each fraction are piped out of the container. When the vapors are cooled, they become liquid again. The liquids formed are the lighter petroleum products, such as gasoline, kerosene, and heating oil. Other refining processes produce different petroleum products, or *petrochemicals*.

Petroleum is one of the most important materials in the modern world. Fuels, such as gasoline, kerosene, and diesel oil, provide the power for automobiles, boats, airplanes, and other vehicles. Fuel oil is burned for heat. Hundreds of other useful products are made from

petroleum, such as perfumes, insecticides, paint thinners, cosmetics, detergents, and explosives.

The Future of Petroleum

New *oil fields* (areas covering petroleum pools) are continually being established and drilled. Yet in spite of these discoveries, petroleum is being used up faster than it is being found. Some scientists predict that the world's petroleum supply will be used up by early next century. Oil can also be extracted from *shale*, a kind of rock, and from tar sands, but getting the oil out of them is very expensive. Scientists are working on new methods of extraction, for these are probably the petroleum sources of the future.

▶▶▶▶ **FIND OUT MORE** ◀◀◀◀
Distillation; Drilling Rig; Fuel; Gasoline; Geology; Kerosene; Natural Gas; Pipeline

PHARAOH

SEE EGYPT, ANCIENT

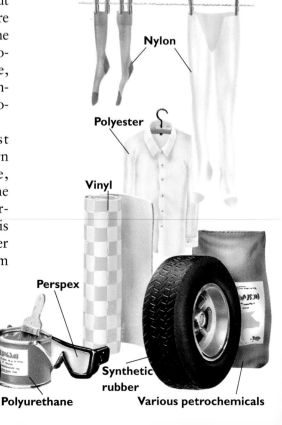

Nylon

Polyester

Vinyl

Ammonia

Polythene

Perspex

Synthetic rubber

▶ A wide range of household and industrial products are made from refining petroleum to produce petroleum products, or petrochemicals.

Various petrochemicals

Vinyl

Polyurethane

Various petrochemicals

PHILADELPHIA

Philadelphia is the largest city in Pennsylvania, and the fifth largest in the United States. Almost six million people live in and around Philadelphia. This city, located where the Schuylkill and Delaware rivers meet, is of great historical importance.

The name, *Philadelphia*, means "brotherly love" in Greek. It was chosen by the city's founder, William Penn, in 1682. Penn and his Society of Friends, called Quakers, planned

the city as a place where people would have freedom in their worship and their daily lives. Philadelphia was the capital of Pennsylvania from 1683 to 1799.

The First and Second Continental Congresses were held in the city, and the Declaration of Independence was signed in Independence Hall in 1776. This historic site is now a national shrine, which also contains the famous Liberty Bell. Nearby is Congress Hall, where the first Continental Congress met.

Philadelphia served as the capital of the United States from 1790 to 1799. Although the seat of government was moved to Washington, Philadelphia continued to expand and prosper. The first bank in the new nation was established in the city. Several industries grew, first in

textiles and clothing, and printing and publishing, and later in metals and machinery. Petroleum products and chemicals were also important industries.

Philadelphia became a great seaport and now has nearly 300 piers and wharves. One of the largest naval bases in the country was built here.

The reputation for religious freedom, associated with Philadelphia since William Penn, attracted many people persecuted in their homelands. The Quakers and refugees from many countries came to make a new life in the city. Many blacks from the southern United States settled here also.

The University of Pennsylvania, founded in 1740, and Temple University are two of the many schools and colleges in Philadelphia and its suburbs. Fairmount Park, a wooded area of more than 3,500 acres (1,416 ha), extends for 10 miles (16 km) and contains the Zoological Gardens, natural settings for summer concerts and plays, and many restored colonial buildings.

▶▶▶▶ **FIND OUT MORE** ◀◀◀◀
Declaration of Independence;
Franklin, Benjamin; Liberty Bell; Penn,
William; Pennsylvania; Society of
Friends

PHILIP, KINGS OF FRANCE

Six kings of France were named Philip.

Philip I (1052–1108) was the son of King Henry I of France. Philip became king in 1060. The French kings at this time ruled only a small territory in the center of France. The rest of the land was controlled by powerful French nobles. In 1066, the

◀ **Elfreth's Alley, one of Philadelphia's older city streets. Many of the streets in the older districts of the city have maintained the style of the 1790s, when Philadelphia was the capital of the United States.**

▲ **Philip I, king of France from 1060 to 1108.**

▲ **Philip IV (the Fair), king of France from 1285 to 1314.**

▶ **Philip VI, king of France from 1328 to 1350.**

Philip II built the huge Escorial palace and church about 30 miles (48 km) from Madrid, Spain. It took 21 years to build, and now contains one of the world's finest collections of paintings, books, and manuscripts. Philip II and most of his successors are buried there.

strongest of these nobles, Duke William of Normandy, invaded England and became its king. He warred with Philip.

Philip II (1165–1223) was the son of King Louis VII of France. He succeeded his father in 1180. A large region of France was controlled by King Henry II of England at this time. But Henry's sons were ready to rebel against their father and to deceive one another. Philip used their quarrels to aid him in winning back most of the English lands in France, including Normandy. Because of this, he was called "Philip Augustus." (Augustus comes from a Latin word meaning "magnificent.") In 1214, Philip won a great victory over the armies of England, Flanders, and the Holy Roman Empire. After that, France was an important power.

Philip Augustus was the first of the French kings to bring most of France under his control. He took power away from the nobles and appointed his own *magistrates* (officials) to oversee each of the French provinces. Philip gave special privileges to the French merchants and encouraged the growth of the cities.

Philip III (1245–1285) was the son of the French king Louis IX, or Saint Louis. Philip succeeded his father in 1270. Louis had been a powerful king and was much loved by the French people. But Philip was weak and spiritless. He depended very much on the advice of others. His uncle, Charles of Anjou, encouraged him to fight an unnecessary war against Aragon, a kingdom in Spain. The French were defeated, and Philip was killed in the final battle.

Philip IV (1268–1314) was known as "The Fair." He succeeded his father, Philip III, in 1285. The most important event in the reign of Philip

IV was his quarrel with Pope Boniface VIII. The Roman Catholic clergy in France had always considered the pope to be their only leader. But Philip now claimed that the king should have the power to collect taxes from the clergy. The quarrel lasted until Boniface died in 1303. Two years later, a French bishop was elected pope. Philip encouraged the new pope to move from Rome to Avignon in France.

Philip V (1294–1322) was the second son of Philip IV. Philip became king after the death of his older brother, Louis X, in 1317. Some people in France claimed that Louis's baby daughter should have been the new ruler. They refused to support Philip. But he strengthened his control over the country by setting up *militias* (small citizen armies) in the cities.

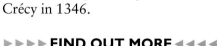

Philip VI (1293–1350) was the grandson of Philip III. He was the first king of the Valois dynasty. Philip became king in 1328. King Edward III of England (the grandson of the French king Philip IV), claimed that he should have been crowned king of France. This quarrel led to the outbreak of the Hundred Years' War between France and England. Edward defeated Philip at the great Battle of Crécy in 1346.

▶▶▶▶ **FIND OUT MORE** ◀◀◀◀
English History; Feudalism; French History; Hundred Years' War; William, Kings of England

PHILIP, KINGS OF SPAIN

Five kings of Spain were named Philip.

Philip I (1478–1506) was called "The Handsome." He was the son of the Holy Roman emperor Maximillian I. In 1499, Philip married Joanna, the daughter of King Ferdinand V and Queen Isabella I of Spain. Ferdinand and Isabella were joint rulers of the two great Spanish kingdoms, Aragon and Castile. When Isabella died in 1504, Philip and Joanna became rulers of Castile. Philip died suddenly at the age of 28.

Philip II (1527–1598) was the son of King Charles I of Spain. Charles was also the Holy Roman emperor. In 1556, Charles *abdicated* (gave up his throne) and broke up his enormous empire. Philip became king of Spain and ruler of the Spanish lands in the Netherlands, Italy, and the Americas. Philip was now the most powerful ruler in Europe. He spent much of his reign fighting rulers of other countries who were jealous of his power. Spain was already at war with France when Philip came to the throne. He defeated the French in two great battles. Philip had married Queen Mary I of England. But after Mary died, a quarrel broke out between Spain and England. Philip, as the most powerful Roman Catholic king, was the defender of the Catholic Church in Europe. The new English queen, Elizabeth I, who was a Protestant, sided with Philip's enemies. In 1588, Philip sent a mighty fleet of ships, called the "Armada," to invade England. But the Spanish ships were destroyed by the English navy and by terrible storms at sea.

When Philip died, Spain's great power was beginning to weaken. Philip's wars had cost vast amounts of money that the country could not afford. Many people lived in terror of the Inquisition, a court that questioned and tortured anyone suspected of being a *heretic* (one who opposes an official religious dogma) or a nonbeliever in the Roman Catholic Church. The Protestants in the Netherlands had rebelled against Spanish rule and were demanding

their independence. Philip had insisted on settling every matter of government himself. He was very hardworking, but his lands were too large to be governed properly by one person alone.

Philip III (1578–1621) succeeded his father, Philip II, in 1598. Unlike his father, Philip was not interested in the business of government. He let his favorite counselors govern Spain.

The Spanish people grew poorer, while the king spent money on festivals and amusements. The Greek painter El Greco was working in Spain during Philip's reign.

Philip IV (1605–1665) succeeded his father, Philip III, in 1621. He, too, left the business of government to his favorite counselors. His main interests were hunting and the arts. The painter Diego Velázquez painted many pictures of Philip IV and his family. The country, meanwhile, grew poorer and weaker. Portugal broke away from Spain and chose its own king. Philip was forced to give the people of the Netherlands their independence.

Philip V (1683–1746) was the grandson of the powerful French king Louis XIV. The Spanish king

▲ Philip II, king of Spain from 1556 to 1598. Philip was 60 years old when he planned the Armada invasion. He carried on his work in his study inside his grand palace of the Escorial near Madrid.

▲ Philip IV, king of Spain from 1621 to 1665.

PHILIPPINES

Capital city
Manila (5,926,000 people, including those in suburbs)

Area
115,831 square miles
(300,000 sq. km)

Population
61,483,000

Government
Multiparty republic

Natural resources
Crude oil, nickel, cobalt, silver, gold, copper, chromite, coal

Export products Electronics, clothes, minerals and ores, farm products, coconut products, timber, petroleum

Unit of money
Peso

Official languages
Pilipino, English

Charles II, who had no children, chose Philip as his successor. But when Charles died in 1700, the rulers of England and the Holy Roman Empire refused to recognize Philip as king of Spain. They were afraid that he would join together the two great kingdoms of France and Spain. This fear provoked a war, the war of the Spanish Succession, in which France and Spain were defeated.

▶▶▶▶ **FIND OUT MORE** ◀◀◀◀
English History; French History; Holy Roman Empire; Netherlands; Portugal; Spanish Armada; Spanish History

PHILIPPINES

The more than 7,000 islands that make up the Philippines stretch out in the western Pacific Ocean about 100 miles (160 km) south of Taiwan, and form the Republic of the Philippines in southern Asia. Borneo is to the southwest. The largest islands are Luzon in the north and Mindanao in the south. Most of the people live on the 11 largest islands. Some of the islands are so small they are not even named. Manila, the chief port and largest city, is the capital.

The islands are the tips of mountains that are partly under the ocean. Earthquakes sometimes shake the islands, and volcanoes erupt. The most recent eruption was Mount Pinatubo in 1991. The climate is humid and warm all year in the lowlands, and cooler in the mountains. *Typhoons* (hurricanes) often strike during the rainy season.

Orchids and other flowers, plants, animals, and birds make the islands a natural wonderland. The coastal waters are full of fish and mollusks, including the pearl oyster. Deposits of chromite, nickel, and copper are among the largest in the

world. Gold and silver are also mined there.

Most of the people live in small villages and make their living from farming. They raise crops of sugarcane, fruits, rice, coconuts, vegetables, and Manila hemp. Valuable timber grows in the mountains.

The people of the Philippines are called Filipinos. During prehistoric times, Malayan peoples came to the islands at different times. They settled in all parts of the islands and developed many speech dialects and local customs. Spanish people arrived in the 1500s, and many Chinese came in later years. Most people speak Pilipino, the national language, which is based on a Malayan dialect called Tagalog. Many people also speak English and Spanish. The Philippines is the only Asian country with a large Christian population.

Ferdinand Magellan, a Portuguese navigator serving Spain, discovered the Philippines on March 14, 1521. Later, Spanish explorers named the islands after Philip II of Spain. In 1898, after the Spanish-American War, the islands were turned over to the United States. William Howard Taft became the first civil governor of the islands. The U.S. Congress passed a bill in 1934 that granted the Philippines independence by 1946. The bill provided for a temporary commonwealth supervised by the United States, but with an elected Philippine president and a constitution. In 1935, the Filipinos adopted a constitution and elected Manuel Quezon as their first president.

In December 1941, Japan invaded and occupied the islands. U.S. forces returned in 1944 and defeated the Japanese the following year. The Philippines gained full independence on July 4, 1946.

Ferdinand Marcos, who was elected president in 1965, restricted the activities of his opponents in the 1970s. In 1986, he was opposed in the presidential elections by Mrs. Corazon Aquino. Marcos won, but the elections proved to be a fraud. Marcos fled the country and Mrs. Aquino became the new president until 1992, when Fidel Ramos was elected president.

▶▶▶▶ **FIND OUT MORE** ◀◀◀◀
Asia; MacArthur, Douglas; Magellan, Ferdinand; Spanish-American War; Taft, William Howard; World War II

 ## PHILOSOPHY

The word *philosophy* comes from two Greek words meaning "love" and "wisdom." A *philosopher*, therefore, is one who loves wisdom enough to spend most of his or her time and energy in search of it. The word "philosophy" is often used to mean a set of basic values and attitudes toward nature, society, and life in general.

Philosophers
Philosophy as a serious study probably began in ancient Greece between 600 and 430 B.C. The ancient Greek philosophers were not satisfied with the mythology of their time. They wanted to explain the nature and origin of the universe through reasoning and observation. The Greek philosophers dealt with many interesting ideas. Among the topics they investigated were politics, beauty, nature, logic, and moral values. The Greek philosophers are one of two important sources of philosophy in the Western world.

◀ **Terraced fields flooded for rice growing in the Philippines.**

▲ **From left to right: Socrates, Pythagoras, Plato, and Aristotle. These famous philosophers laid down some of the first theories of life. Their work is still discussed and studied today.**

Philosophers will often ponder the oddest questions. It is said that two famous thirteenth-century philosophers, St. Thomas Aquinas and Albert the Great, used to argue for hours about how many angels could sit on the point of a pin.

The other major source is the ancient Hebrew prophets. The writings of these prophets and the history of the Hebrew people are recorded in the Bible. Many of the same questions that occupied the Greek philosophers are discussed in the Bible. Together, the Greek (Hellenic) and Israelite (Hebraic) writers formed the beginning of philosophy in the Western world. Most important Western philosophical ideas can be traced to one of these two sources.

As time passed and the world changed, so did philosophy. In the Middle Ages, philosophy was dominated by the Catholic Church. During that time, philosophers, notably St. Thomas Aquinas, were concerned with the conflict between faith and

▼ French philosophers including Voltaire and Diderot, enlightened thinkers of the Age of Reason (mid-1800s).

reason. With the Renaissance, philosophy turned from the supernatural to the natural for explanations of the external world. During the 1600s, philosophers became more daring in their thinking. They believed that people should question all established ideas. On this basis, philosophers constructed many new views of the world and of human kind's place in it.

The German philosopher Immanuel Kant believed that reality extends far beyond what a person's five senses tell him or her, but that a

person's knowledge of reality cannot extend further than the senses. He also believed that the existence of God was proved by the existence of nature. (All the things in the natural world must have been created by someone, and people call the creator God.) The English philosopher John Locke influenced political thought with his belief that all people have certain basic rights that their governments should protect.

In the Eastern nations of China and India, philosophy is as old as it is in the West. Two of the most important Chinese philosophers were Confucius and Lao Tzu. Confucius taught that people should be kind to one another and respect their elders. Lao Tzu encouraged people to follow the course of nature and live simply. Eastern philosophy is closely tied to religion. It contains many wise sayings and much advice on the best way to live. It is only in recent times that Western thinkers have discovered the great wisdom of Eastern philosophy.

Some Philosophical Questions
For thousands of years, people have sought answers to several basic philosophical questions.

AESTHETICS. Think of something that seems beautiful to you. It might be something from nature, such as a flower or snow on a branch. Or it might be something artistic, such as a poem, a song, a painting, or a piece of sculpture. Now ask yourself, "What makes this seem beautiful to me?" Many philosophers have dealt with this question and others like it. Some find beauty in order and precision, others in the pleasures experienced through the senses. Still others find beauty in the ideas that a work of art contains. This area of study is known as *aesthetics*.

METAPHYSICS AND EPISTEMOLOGY. Sometimes we may feel that what we see is not all there is to the universe—and that there is more to it than even the most powerful

▲ John Locke, English philosopher.

telescopes and microscopes can reveal. Metaphysics attempts to understand the nature of ultimate reality—a reality of which we see only a small part—through reasoning. But we must understand *how* we look at reality and think about it, since we distort reality, or fail to see it entirely, in our looking and thinking. The study of the origin, nature, and methods of knowledge is known as *epistemology*.

ETHICS. The area of philosophy that tries to determine what is right and wrong is known as *ethics*. It tries to answer the question, "How does a good and honorable person act?" There are many views on what the ethical person should do, but they all concern a person's responsibility—to oneself, to one's country, or to one's God. Some ethical standards have even been made into laws in an effort to make people behave honorably.

Everyone is a philosopher to some degree, because an important part of growing up is developing a personal philosophy. Each person eventually has to decide what mankind is, why he or she exists, and what is right and wrong in his or her own life and in life in general.

▶▶▶▶ **FIND OUT MORE** ◀◀◀◀
Aristotle; Confucius; Jewish History; Plato; Religion; Socrates

PHOENICIA

Phoenicia was an ancient region in the Middle East. It extended for about 200 miles (320 km) along the eastern coast of the Mediterranean Sea. Most of Phoenicia is now the modern country of Lebanon. The Phoenicians were great seafarers and traders. They were known throughout the ancient world for the reddish purple dye that they made from a type of *mollusk* (shellfish). Their most important invention was an alphabet. This alphabet was copied by the Greeks with whom the Phoenicians traded. It eventually developed into the alphabet that we use today.

Phoenicia was made up of self-ruling city-states. Its two greatest cities were Sidon and Tyre. (Phoenicians are called Sidonites in the Bible.) Phoenicia was originally ruled by Egypt. But the Phoenicians rebelled, and by 900 B.C., they had won their independence. Phoenician traders sailed to ports all over the Mediterranean. They even ventured into the Atlantic Ocean, possibly sailing as far as England. Phoenicia founded several colonies, including Carthage in North Africa. In the 700s B.C., a series of foreign invasions of Phoenicia began. Phoenicia was conquered by the Assyrians and then the Persians. The Greek general Alexander the Great invaded Phoenicia in 332 B.C. He besieged Tyre for seven months before the city surrendered. In 64 B.C., Phoenicia was made a part of the Roman Empire.

▶ **The Phoenicians were skilled craft workers. They were famous for their ivory carvings, like this head of a girl.**

▶▶▶▶ **FIND OUT MORE** ◀◀◀◀
Alexander the Great; Alphabet; Carthage; Lebanon

PHOENIX

SEE ANIMALS OF MYTH AND LEGEND

PHONOGRAPH

SEE RECORDING

WHERE TO DISCOVER MORE

Marston, Elsa. *Lebanon: New Light in an Ancient Land.* New York: Macmillan, 1994.

Foster, L.M. *Lebanon.* Chicago: Childrens Press, 1992.

◀ **The Phoenicians invented the process of glass-blowing. This is a colored glass perfume bottle.**

The Phoenicians were famous for the reddish purple dye that they produced. This dye was made from the glands of the murex sea snail.

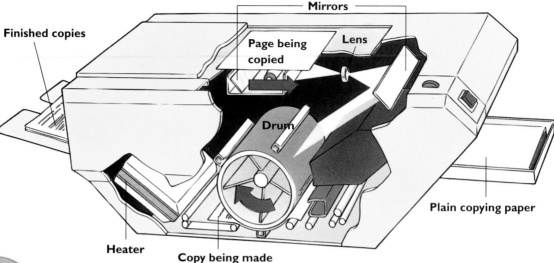

▶ A diagram to show the different parts of a photocopier, and how the process works to produce the finished copies.

Finished copies

Mirrors

Page being copied

Lens

Drum

Plain copying paper

Heater

Copy being made

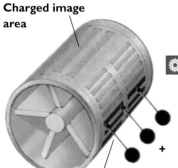

Charged image area

Toner dust attracted to charged image area

+

▲ The rotating drum of a photocopier. Toner sticks to the area on the drum that is charged with static electricity. The electrical charges correspond to the image that is being copied. As the paper passes under the drum, it picks up the toner particles that make up the image. The toner is dried before the finished copy comes out.

⚙ PHOTOCOPIER

A *photocopier* is a machine that can copy a picture, a page of a book, or a letter in seconds. Before photocopiers were invented, there was no way of making quick copies. People had to write out a page, trace a drawing by hand, or make a carbon copy of a letter using inked paper.

When you press the button on a photocopier, a bright light goes on inside. It lights up the page or drawing. A lens inside the machine projects an image of the page or picture onto a metal drum.

This drum is electrified so that its surface has an electric charge all over it. When the image is projected onto it, the light in the bright parts of the image destroys the electric charge. Only the dark parts of the drum are still electrified.

A black powder, called *toner,* is dusted over the drum. It clings only to the parts of the surface that are electrified. When a sheet of paper is pressed against the drum, the powder comes off and an image of the page or picture forms on the paper. This process is called *xerography.*

Fax machines also produce copies of pages. They send signals to each other through a telephone line. One machine can copy a page or drawing "scanned" by the first machine.

⚙ PHOTOELECTRICITY

When leaving a large supermarket, you may have passed through a door that opened for you automatically. You didn't have to push the door or touch it in any way. The door may have been opened by an *electric eye,* which is a device operated by photo-electricity.

How Photoelectricity Works

Photoelectricity is a type of electric power produced by light. Light is a form of energy. Certain metals, such as cesium and potassium, give off electrons when struck by light. These metals are called "light-sensitive." Electric eyes, which are also called "photo-tubes" or "photoelectric cells," contain light-sensitive metal plates. So, when light strikes an electric eye, electrons are produced. These electrons form a weak electric current, which can be amplified to work a switch.

In the case of the automatic door, an electric eye is attached to one side of the passageway. A thin beam of light shines across the passageway onto the electric eye. When a person cuts the beam, he or she interrupts the light rays. This sets off the switch that opens the door.

Photoelectricity is used to produce power for many other machines. Some burglar alarms, for example, use electric eyes. If a burglar passes through a door where light is shining on an electric eye, an alarm will go off. Street lights turn on automatically by means of electric eyes. Motion picture projectors use photoelectricity to produce sound.

▶▶▶▶ **FIND OUT MORE** ◀◀◀◀
Battery; Electricity;
Electric Power; Light

PHOTOGRAPHY

Have you ever thought about the many ways photography is used? Newspapers, magazines, and books are filled with photographs. Posters, shop window displays, and advertisements all make use of photographs. Tiny strips of microfilm record the printed pages of books, newspapers, and other materials. We use photocopying machines to make photographic copies of letters and other documents. X-ray photography is used in medicine and industry. Remote-controlled cameras in spacecrafts photograph distant planets.

Taking Photographs
There are all kinds of cameras, and some are very expensive. Yet a simple camera and film are all you need to take a photograph. Most cameras fall into two categories:

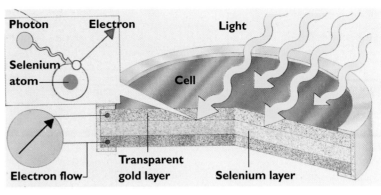

reflex and nonreflex. A nonreflex camera has a direct-vision viewfinder for viewing, framing, and perhaps even bringing the subject into focus. A reflex camera allows you to view and focus on the subject through the lens using a mirror and prism system inside the camera. Many popular 35mm single-lens reflex (SLR) cameras come into this category. More advanced are large-format SLR and twin-lens reflex (TLR) cameras. For professional studio work, many photographers prefer a large bellows camera.

Small pocket cameras use cartridge film that is easy to insert and remove. Most 35mm cameras use either cassette or roll film. Bellows cameras use sheet film. And there are also throwaway cameras, bought ready-loaded with film, which are thrown away after the film has been exposed and developed.

▲ **One type of photoelectric cell is made of the semimetallic element *selenium*. It releases electrons when light (photons) shines on it, and the flow of electrons makes an electric current.**

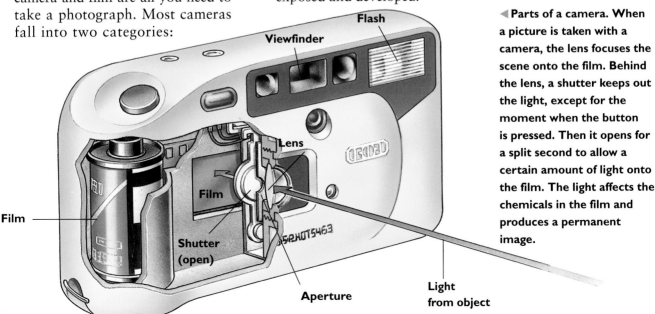

◀**Parts of a camera. When a picture is taken with a camera, the lens focuses the scene onto the film. Behind the lens, a shutter keeps out the light, except for the moment when the button is pressed. Then it opens for a split second to allow a certain amount of light onto the film. The light affects the chemicals in the film and produces a permanent image.**

▲ By using a long exposure and moving the camera, a photographer can "paint" a picture on film. Here, a surrealistic image has been created from traffic lights.

With a modern camera, all you have to do is aim the camera at your subject and press the button that opens the shutter. Light enters the camera through the lens when the shutter snaps open, and this produces a chemical change on the film. This is called *exposing* the film.

Each type of film has a particular sensitivity to light. This is called the *film speed*. You can find a film's speed from the ASA (American Standards Association) or ISO (International Standards Organization) numbers on the film and its carton. These numbers are interchangeable—they mean the same thing, whether they are called ASA or ISO. For example, 50 ASA, or ISO, is slow (the film needs long exposure in poor light but is good for detail); 200 to 400 ASA, or ISO, is fast (good in most lights and can "freeze" a fast-moving subject).

Using the viewfinder on your camera, you can adjust your position to take the kind of picture you want. It is important to hold the camera steady when taking a picture. Moving the camera will blur the image on the film. Always advance the film after taking a picture. If you expose the same piece of film twice, you will get a double image—one image on top of another.

Aim your camera so that sunlight does not shine directly at the lens. Direct sunlight produces unwanted reflections and glare in the finished photograph. If you are taking photographs indoors, or where the light is not strong, you will need a flash attachment or some other bright light source.

Developing Photographs

Most people have the exposed films developed professionally. Some people enjoy developing their own film. Developing must be done in a totally dark room. If light should strike the film before it is developed, your photographs will be ruined. Darkrooms can be lit with a safe light (usually a special red light bulb) that will not damage the film.

Exposed film is first placed in a developer solution. The developer makes a chemical change on the film that brings out a negative image. The *negative* is a transparent, backward version of your original picture. The lighter areas show up dark on the negative, and the darker areas come out light.

LEARN BY DOING

Once you have some skill at taking good, sharp photographs, you can try some special effects with your camera. Try adjusting the light for an indoor photograph so that the light hits your subject from an unusual angle—from one side, from above, from below. Take several pictures of the same subject, changing the direction of the light each time. The various light directions will produce many different moods, even though the subject remains the same.

Even if your camera does not have an adjustable lens, different effects can be achieved by turning the camera. Try taking pictures of the same object, turning your camera so that the view is wide or long or at an angle. Close-up shots make interesting photographs. Try some close-up views of a person, a leaf, a reflection, a crack in the sidewalk, a doorknob, the spokes of a bicycle wheel, or anything you think looks interesting.

You can produce some interesting photographs by aiming your camera from an unusual angle. You might photograph a tree by lying down underneath it and pointing your camera right up into the branches. You can also frame your subject by shooting a picture through a window, door, archway, or grove of trees so that the window, archway, or trees surround the edges of your picture. Take some action shots of a moving subject by setting the shutter at high speed.

▲ A fantastic stop-action close-up photograph of a bee.

PROCESSING BLACK-AND-WHITE FILM

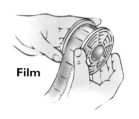

Developer

Stop bath

Fixer

Film

Water

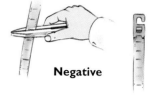

Negative

▲ The film is taken out of its case and wrapped around a special holder. This is done in a dark room.

▲ The film is put inside a tank. Chemicals are added one at a time for carefully measured periods of time.

▲ The film is then washed to remove the chemicals after they have done their specific jobs.

▲ The film is hung up to dry. The images that are developed from the film are called negatives.

PRINTING BLACK-AND-WHITE FILM

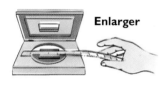

Enlarger

Lens

Developer

Stop bath

Fixer

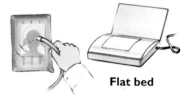

Photographic paper

Flat bed

▲ The negative is placed on a holder below the lens of an enlarger.

▲ Light is shone through the negative onto photographic paper below.

▲ The print is then developed and fixed in the same way as the film.

▲ The print is washed then placed on a heated metal flat bed or hung up to dry.

After the negative image is fully developed, the film is placed in a tank containing a stopper solution, then the film is rinsed with cool water to wash off the chemicals. The developing process must always be timed. If film is left in the developer solution too long, the pictures turn almost black. After being washed, the film is placed in a solution called "hypo" (short for hyposulfite). This is a mixture of chemicals that hardens the film and fixes the image to make it ready for printing.

Printing Photographs

In printing a photograph, the negative image is used to make a *positive* image. The negative is pressed tightly against a sheet of special paper that is sensitive to light. When light is directed through the negative to the paper, a chemical change takes place on the paper. The paper is developed, fixed, and washed to finally produce the photograph.

Small photographs can be enlarged by projecting the negative through an enlarger, which has a lens that makes the image bigger, just as a slide projector can enlarge small pictures by projecting them onto a screen. The enlarger projects the magnified image onto light-sensitive paper. When the paper is developed, an enlarged print comes out.

An instant camera, such as a Polaroid, uses a special film that does not produce a regular negative. The undeveloped print is ejected from the camera just seconds after you snap the picture. It develops right in front of your eyes.

Color film for regular cameras comes in two types. Color-negative film produces a negative from which a print can be made. The other type produces transparencies, or slides, which are made on a piece of film, instead of being printed on paper. Transparencies must be held up to a light, or projected onto a screen, in order to be seen.

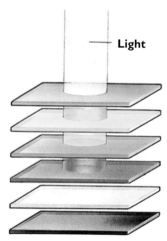

Light

▲ Color film is made up of six layers. The first is an emulsion that records blue light, the second absorbs excess blue light, the third records green light, and the fourth records red light. The fifth, a plastic base, supports the emulsions. The last layer is a special backing that absorbs any remaining light.

▲ Joseph Nicéphore Niépce, a French pioneer of photography. He is usually credited with taking the very first photographs.

▶ The daguerreotype camera, invented in 1839 by the French painter, Louis J.M. Daguerre.

▲ George Eastman, who founded the Kodak company.

QUIZ

1. What kind of film do most 35mm cameras use?
2. Which is faster: 50 ASA or 200 ASA film?
3. What is a film's negative?
4. What are the two types of color film used for regular cameras?
5. In what year did Eastman develop the lightweight camera?

(Answers on page 2176)

History of Photography

The earliest known photograph was made in 1826 by a French chemist, Joseph N. Niépce. He placed a light-sensitive metal plate in a camera, set the camera on a windowsill, and left the shutter open for eight hours. It took eight hours to get an image on the plate because the chemicals were very slow in reacting to light.

Since that first photograph, faster and more accurate films have been developed. Louis Daguerre invented a way of making positive images right on the metal plates used in the camera. These metal photographs (called *daguerreotypes*) were very popular. *Tintypes* were another kind of metal photograph that produced a negative image against a black background. The black background made the negative look like a positive image.

The first flexible film, made of celluloid plastic, was invented in 1887 by George Eastman. In 1888, he made a simple camera that was lightweight and easy to use. These two inventions made photography a popular hobby for everyone. People began taking "snapshots" of themselves, the places they visited, and of practically everything else. The

invention of reliable color film in 1935 added even more to the enjoyment of photography.

Careers in Photography

Many people have jobs in photography. Professional photographers may take pictures of famous people, models, buildings, wildlife, or family weddings. Press photographers take pictures for newspapers and magazines.

In the TV and movie world, there are careers for cameramen, cinematographers, technicians, and editors. Also, photography is now widely used in many branches of science, including medicine. Many colleges offer courses in photography and film production.

▶▶▶▶ **FIND OUT MORE** ◀◀◀◀
Camera; Microfilm; Motion Picture; Photocopier; Television

⚙ PHOTOSYNTHESIS

Green plants make their own food. They take in water and carbon dioxide and produce sugar. This food-making process is called *photosynthesis*. For photosynthesis to take place, green plants must be exposed to light.

Air, which includes carbon dioxide

LEARN BY DOING

There is a definite art to taking good photographs. All too often holiday snapshots show the people too far away. All you see are a few stone columns and some tiny figures. This does not make an interesting picture. To avoid doing this yourself, remember to keep the buildings at a distance. This way you can get most of them into the picture. But do the opposite with the people: Keep them near the camera—9 feet (3 m) is about the right distance. If you do this, you can still see the building in the background.

gas, enters a plant through *stomata* (tiny holes) in the surfaces of its leaves. Water is taken into a plant through its roots. The water rises up the stem to the leaves, and there the water and carbon dioxide combine and form sugar. This combination is a *chemical reaction*. Chemical reactions cannot take place without energy. The energy in photosynthesis comes from light. This light energy is stored in *chlorophyll*—the green substance that gives most plants their color. Chlorophyll causes the reaction.

Photosynthesis takes place in many complicated steps. But the process can be divided into two basic parts. In the first part, chlorophyll causes water to break up into hydrogen and oxygen. Oxygen passes out of the plant through small openings in the leaves. In the second part of photosynthesis, hydrogen combines with carbon dioxide to form sugar.

Plants change the sugar into other food materials. The main one is starch, which is stored in a plant's roots. Fats and proteins are also produced. All animals eat either plants or other animals that eat plants. So photosynthesis is one of the most important activities in nature.

▶▶▶▶ **FIND OUT MORE** ◀◀◀◀
Air; Chemistry; Hydrogen; Oxygen; Plant; Tree

PHYSICAL EDUCATION

The term "physical education" covers a broad range of activities, from teaching and coaching sports and games to helping people with crippling diseases to exercise properly. Physical education specialists begin their studies in college, where they take courses in human anatomy, biology, nutrition, and *hygiene* (health and disease prevention). They take part in sports and games where they learn body strengthening and exercise techniques, as well as teamwork and sportsmanship.

Students who plan to become teachers of physical education take special courses to learn how to teach. They study the growth and development of the human body so they will know which sports and games are best suited to people of various ages. They learn safety and first-aid techniques in order to prevent accidents during games and to be able to help anyone who may get injured. Students also study game rules and learn to handle the equipment used in a wide variety of sports activities.

Physical education teachers work in elementary, junior high, high schools, and colleges. They are employed in camps, playgrounds, and community recreation centers. Physical education

Photosynthesis is possible because a leaf exposes a lot of moist cells to the air in order to take in carbon dioxide. But this also means that the leaf loses water by evaporation. In one summer day, a tree may lose water weighing about five times as much as its own leaves. In temperate climates, as much water is lost from plants in this way as flows out to the sea from rivers.

▼ It is important to look after your health. Exercise is a good and enjoyable way to keep your body fit and trim. There are many sporting activities you can do. You will learn about these in your physical education classes at school. This boy is playing baseball.

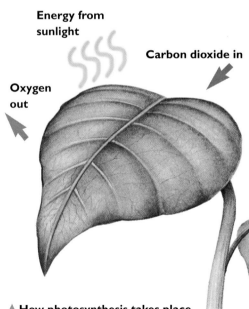

Energy from sunlight

Carbon dioxide in

Oxygen out

Water from roots

▲ How photosynthesis takes place. Water enters the plant through root hairs. It passes through the stem and into the veins of the leaves. Some of the water is given off as vapor. The rest combines with carbon dioxide to make sugar, which the plant uses as food.

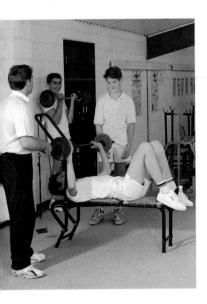

▲ These boys are being taught the correct way to use free weights. It is very easy to pull a muscle in the arms and legs or damage the spine if sports equipment is used incorrectly.

▶ The Concorde is a good example of aerodynamics at work. Its streamline shape is effective at reducing drag caused by airflow.

▲ Aerodynamics studies how objects behave when they move through the air. A paper plane flies through the air because its wings give it lift.

specialists are employed by the military and by police departments. Since exercising has been proven to reduce stress in people, large corporations often have exercise and recreational facilities in their buildings. Physical education specialists frequently direct exercise programs for company employees.

Everyone in the field of physical education must work closely with other people. For this reason, most physical education specialists receive training in psychology and in *group dynamics* (how people in a group or team get along together). A physical education teacher may find a child who is afraid to play certain sports. The teacher must find out why the child is afraid, and try to help him or her. A physical therapist helping patients improve their physical condition can also help them overcome depression and unhappiness. If you should decide on a career in physical education, you will be helping other people to live healthier lives.

PHYSICS

Have you ever wondered what happens when you turn on a flashlight? How does the electricity in the battery turn into a beam of light? What makes an airplane fly? Why is it that a piece of wood floats, but a piece of iron sinks? To find answers, you must go to the science of physics. Physicists study and experiment with *matter* and *energy* in order to find out how things work.

Matter
Sand, plastic, glass, steam, wood, metal, milk, and cloth are all substances that you know. There are many other substances in the world,

and all of them together are called matter. Matter has two *properties*, or characteristics. All matter has the property of *mass* (it offers resistance to any force that tries to move it) and the property of *volume* (it takes up space). A tiny grain of sand or a microscopic atom both have mass—even though the mass is very small. You cannot put two atoms or grains of sand in exactly the same place at the same time. They both have volume, and so they cannot both use the same space at the same time.

Energy
Physicists study matter to find out how it is built and how it reacts to energy. The ability to work, or move in some way, is called *energy*. Eight basic forms of energy are heat, electricity, light, sound, mechanical (potential or kinetic), nuclear, chemical, and magnetic.

Heat energy is used to operate steam engines, to cook food, to warm houses, and to do many other things. *Electric energy* is used for producing light and for running all kinds of machines. A photographer uses *light energy* for taking pictures. When you speak, you use *sound energy* to make others hear you. When you pedal a bicycle, you use *mechanical energy* to make the wheels move. *Nuclear energy* is used to explode atom bombs, produce electric power for cities, and drive ships. *Chemical energy* holds together the molecules of chemical compounds. *Magnetic energy* lifts certain metals against the force of gravity.

Physics is the study of nature, and the first scientists to study physics were known as natural philosophers. Mostly, they guessed how things happened. For instance, the Greeks guessed that matter was made of atoms. In this case, they were right, but guesswork was often wildly wrong. Today, physicists work by theory and experiment; they work out a theory, often using advanced mathematics, and then they test if the theory is correct by carrying out experiments. The need to carry out precise experiments made it necessary to have accurate systems of weights and measures, and accurate instruments to do the weighing and measuring.

Today, when you study physics, you learn how matter and energy work together. Through a knowledge of physics, people have been able to produce all kinds of machines from simple can openers to very complicated computers and rocket systems. Astrophysicists study outer space and the movements of planets, stars, and galaxies. Nuclear physicists study the tiny, but extremely powerful, atom and its parts.

▶▶▶▶ FIND OUT MORE ◀◀◀◀

Elements of Physics see Atom; Color; Cryogenics; Electricity; Energy; Fire; Fluid; Friction; Gas; Gear; Gravity and Gravitation; Heat and Cold; Light; Liquid; Machine; Magnet; Matter; Measurement; Motion; Nuclear Energy; Orbit; Perpetual Motion; Photoelectricity; Radiation; Radioactivity; Relativity; Solid; Sound; Space; Spectrum; Vacuum; Wave; Weight; X Ray

Physicists see Archimedes; Bacon, Roger; Bohr, Niels; Copernicus, Nicolaus; Curie Family; Einstein, Albert; Faraday, Michael; Fermi, Enrico; Galileo Galilei; Galvani, Luigi; Newton, Sir Isaac; Planck, Max

Products of Physics see Computer; Diesel Engine; Electric Power; Electronics; Engine; Geiger Counter; Gyroscope; Jet Propulsion; Lasers and Masers; Motor; Pendulum; Pump; Radar; Radio; Rocket; Scale; Television; Temperature Scale

---

MAJOR FIELDS OF STUDY IN PHYSICS

Mechanics

Forces and motion, and how they affect matter. Includes *fluid mechanics*, the study of liquids and gases, and *solid mechanics*, the study of solids. Solid mechanics can be divided into *statics*, the study of bodies at rest, and *dynamics*, the study of bodies in motion. A similar division can be made for fluid mechanics.

Optics

Light: what it is, how it behaves, and how it can be used.

Thermodynamics

Heat: how it can be used, and how it changes to and from other forms of energy.

Acoustics

Sound: how it is produced, transmitted, and received. Includes *ultrasonics*, the study of sound waves that are too high-pitched to be heard by human beings.

Electricity and Magnetism

Electrical charges and magnetic forces and effects. These are closely related because an electric current produces a magnetic field, and a magnetic field can produce an electric current. Includes *electronics*, the study of electrons and how they move.

Atomic, Molecular, and Nuclear Physics

Atomic physics is the study of atoms as a whole. Molecular physics is the study of atoms in groups, molecules. Nuclear physics is the study of *nuclei*, the hard inner core of atoms, and the study of the nature of subatomic particles and other tiny bits of matter.

Solid-State Physics

The physical properties of solids, especially crystals.

Cryogenics

Extremely low temperatures and their effects, including *superconductivity*.

▶ **Physics involves the study of many everyday objects, their effects, and their applications. The principles of physics are used in everyday life. For example, the simple mechanics of levers are applied in cranes used in industry.**

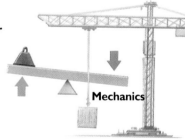

Mechanics

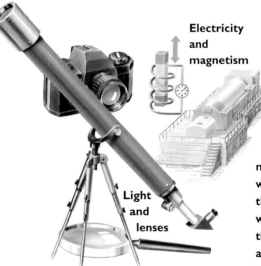

Electricity and magnetism

Light and lenses

◀ **Light and lenses, and electricity and magnetism are two branches of physics. Electricity generators use the principle of moving a magnet in a coil of wire. The way light passes through glass affects how we see objects—whether through a magnifying glass, a camera lens, or a telescope.**

The piano has changed very little since the 1860s. People have experimented with different shapes, two keyboards, pedal boards, and electronic reproduction, but none of these have caught on for the concert platform.

PHYSIOLOGY

SEE HUMAN BODY

 ## PIANO

The piano is probably the best known of all Western musical instruments. Pianos are used in chamber and symphony orchestras. Singers, instrumental musicians, and dancers often use piano accompaniment. There are pianos in many homes and most schools.

The largest pianos are the concert grands, which are about 9 feet (3 m) in length, and the baby grands, about 5 feet (1.5 m) in length. Both have wing-shaped bodies and are used mostly by serious and professional musicians. Console or spinet pianos are most often found in homes and schools. Their bodies are compact, and they fit easily in small spaces or against a wall. Upright pianos are similar to consoles, but they are taller.

The piano is a combination percussion and stringed instrument, operated by a *keyboard*. The keyboard consists of 88 white and black keys. Ask someone to play some notes on a piano while you look inside. Each key controls a felt-covered *hammer* inside the piano. When you press a key, a hammer moves up and strikes a set of two or three wire strings. Each set of strings is tuned to a particular pitch, so that each piano key sounds a different note. The low-pitched keys are on the left side of the keyboard, the high-pitched keys are on the right.

As you press a key, the hammer rises and at the same time the *damper* moves away from the strings. The damper is a small, felt-covered piece of wood that rests on a set of strings to keep them from vibrating and producing a tone. The damper stays on the strings until a key is pressed. Then it moves off the strings so that the hammer can hit the strings and make a tone. When you release the key, the damper falls back onto the strings and silences the tone. If you press a key and hold it down, the hammer will hit the strings and then move back a short way allowing them to vibrate.

Underneath the piano keyboard near the floor are a set of foot pedals. The damper pedal on the right raises all the dampers inside the piano. This lets all the strings vibrate freely and allows tones to overlap—keep on sounding while other tones are being played. The soft pedal on the left shifts all the hammers to one side so that they strike only one string in each set. This produces a softer tone. Some pianos have a third pedal between the other two called the *sostenuto*, or sustaining, pedal. This pedal releases dampers on only those keys that are pressed down and then released by the pianist.

The piano was first invented about 1709 by an Italian harpsichord maker named Bartolommeo Cristofori. He wanted to combine in one instrument the delicate sound of the *harpsichord* and the power of the *clavichord*. These two keyboard instruments were popular in the 1600s and 1700s. Harpsichord tones are produced by quills that pluck the strings. Clavichord tones are made

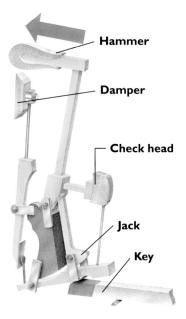

Hammer

Damper

Check head

Jack

Key

▲ The action of a piano is based on a lever movement by the key, which is transmitted to a felt-covered hammer that strikes the piano string. A damper prevents the note from sounding after the key is released.

▼ A piano keyboard.

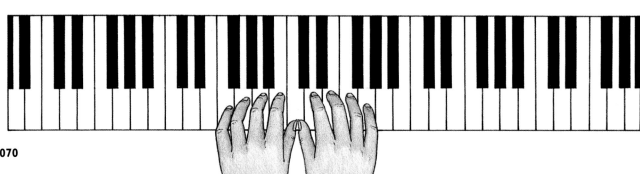

by leather pieces that rub the strings. Cristofori's first piano had leather-covered hammers that hit the strings. The loudness or softness of the tone depended on how hard the player hit the keys. The word "piano" is an abbreviation of the Italian word *pianoforte,* meaning "soft-loud." The instrument was given this name to describe its variety of sounds.

In the 1760s, Johann Christian Bach (a son of Johann Sebastian Bach) performed a series of concerts on the piano. This gave many people a chance to hear the new instrument, and by the beginning of the 1800s, the piano had become very popular. Through the years, improvements were made in the tone quality and pitch of the piano.

▶▶▶▶ **FIND OUT MORE** ◀◀◀◀
Bach Family; Music; Musical Instruments; Percussion Instruments; Stringed Instruments

◀ **This piano was given to the German composer Ludwig van Beethoven in 1818 by its maker, Thomas Broadwood.**

over a half century, he was to be a great leader in the visual arts.

Picasso's talents were varied. He not only painted pictures and murals, but he also did sculpture and even designed stage costumes and scenery. Unlike most painters, he did not develop one particular style of painting. He would paint one way for a few years, then change his style so much that the new work would look like that of a different person!

Soon after arriving in Paris from Spain, he went through his "blue period" (1901–1904). He painted sad figures and mournful faces in gloomy shades of blue and gray. Perhaps he was lonely for Spain. Then he moved into his "circus period,"

It is said that Picasso could draw before he could talk. At the age of 14, he spent one day on an art school test that most people needed a month to complete. By age 16, he had passed all the tests that Spain's art schools could offer.

PICASSO, PABLO
(1881–1973)

As a young boy in Spain, Pablo Picasso could draw amazingly well. A portrait he did of his father looked like the work of a grown artist, but Picasso was in his early teens when he drew it. He was not quite 20 years old when he left Spain for Paris. Almost at once, he was a success as an artist—selling pictures and even having an exhibition of his work. Soon Picasso was in the middle of the exciting modern art movement in Paris. For well

◀ **Picasso painted this portrait of his mother when he was only 14 years old.**

▲ *Acrobat with a Ball*, by Pablo Picasso.

when he created the painting shown here—*Acrobat with a Ball*. Picasso loved the circus and the make-believe that went with it. Once a week he would go to the part of Paris where the circus people lived to paint clowns, acrobats, and bareback riders. In the painting, he has caught the graceful acrobat in the delicate act of balancing on a big ball. This is contrasted with the powerful wall of muscle and strength in the back and silhouette of the other figure.

Next, Picasso went into his "rose period"—a pink, happy time, as shown in his canvases from those years. You can read in the article on MODERN ART about the next period that Picasso was involved in—the development of *cubism*, a very important era in modern art history. Picasso continued to change his styles.

▲ The artist Pablo Picasso, with a piece of his sculpture.

Pierrot with Mask, Picasso dressed Paulo in the floppy costume of the famous French pantomime figure.

One of Picasso's best-known paintings is *Guernica*, done in 1937 during the Spanish Civil War. Nazi airplanes had bombed the Spanish town of Guernica. Picasso was outraged by news of the death and destruction and put these feelings into a painting 26 feet (8 m) long. It is painted in black, white, and gray, and shows people dying and suffering in the raid.

Picasso became famous and wealthy. His pictures sold for large amounts of money in his lifetime. Some of his little drawings attained fame, such as his *Dove of Peace*, a sketch of a neighbor's pigeon that has become known the world over as a peace symbol. In his long, productive life, Picasso experimented with many new ways of painting, always searching for new forms of visual expression. He greatly admired the curved shapes of African sculpture. This admiration was reflected in his own paintings and sculptures. Picasso was a very influential artist, and his work changed the course of modern art. He is considered the most famous artist of this century.

▶▶▶▶ **FIND OUT MORE** ◀◀◀◀
Modern Art

PICCARD, AUGUSTE AND JACQUES

SEE DEEP-SEA LIFE, OCEAN

PICTURE WRITING

SEE HIEROGLYPHICS, WRITTEN LANGUAGE

▲ *Bullfight*, painted in 1934, expresses Pablo Picasso's fascination with color and experimental form.

One of Picasso's favorite subjects for many years was his son, Paulo. He first sketched him on the day he was born, and he continued to sketch and paint pictures of the boy while he grew up. In one painting, *Paulo as*

PIERCE, FRANKLIN
(1804–1869)

Franklin Pierce, the fourteenth President of the United States, served during a time when the country was expanding westward and increasing its population with thousands of immigrants. It was also a period when bitter feelings were developing between the North and South that would lead to the Civil War.

Pierce was born in Hillsboro, New Hampshire. His father, General Benjamin Pierce, had been an officer during the Revolutionary War and governor of New Hampshire. Franklin attended Bowdoin College in Maine, and graduated third in his class in 1824. A college friend, the writer Nathaniel Hawthorne, once spoke of Pierce's "fascination of manner" that lay "deep in the kindness of his nature."

After studying law, Pierce served in the United States House of Representatives and in the Senate. At the start of the Mexican War, he enlisted as a private, but soon became a brigadier general. In 1852, he was elected President by a large majority over his former military commander, General Winfield Scott.

During Pierce's administration, the United States, through the Gadsden Purchase in 1853, bought a tract of land from Mexico. The purchase, which added land to the southern borders of Arizona and New Mexico, completed the continental expansion of the United States. In 1854, Pierce influenced the Senate to ratify a trade treaty with Japan, which had been arranged by Commodore Matthew C. Perry of the U.S. Navy.

Pierce tried to settle differences between the North and the South and included people from both sections in his Cabinet. When Pierce signed the Kansas-Nebraska Act, a law passed by Congress in 1854, many of his admirers turned against him. The act created new territories, Kansas and Nebraska, out of Native American lands in the West. It stated that settlers in each territory would decide for themselves whether to allow slavery. This law made it possible for slavery to spread and thus helped create conflict between people who wanted slavery and those who did not. The Northern Democrats refused to nominate Pierce for a second term. Pierce opposed slavery himself, but he feared the unity of the nation was at stake.

Four years after Pierce returned to New Hampshire, the Civil War began. He was bitterly opposed to it, and believed it was a tragedy that could have been prevented.

►►►► **FIND OUT MORE** ◄◄◄◄
Kansas; Mexican War; Nebraska; Perry, Oliver and Matthew

**FRANKLIN PIERCE
FOURTEENTH
PRESIDENT**

**MARCH 4, 1853–
MARCH 3, 1857**

Born: November 23, 1804, Hillsborough (now Hillsboro), New Hampshire
Parents: General Benjamin Pierce and Anna Kendrick Pierce
Education: Bowdoin College
Religion: Episcopalian
Occupation: Lawyer
Political party: Democratic
State represented: New Hampshire
Married: 1834 to Jane Appleton (1806–1863)
Children: 3 sons (one died in childhood)
Died: October 8, 1869, Concord, New Hampshire
Buried: Concord, New Hampshire

◄ Franklin Pierce supported the Kansas-Nebraska Act, which caused heated discussions and violence among the people of Kansas and Nebraska.

▲ A domestic sow with her litter of piglets. The smallest and weakest piglet in a litter is known as the *runt*.

▲ Domestic pigs are descended from the wild boar, a woodland animal with a bristly coat and sharp curving tusks.

PIG

The pig, considered to be one of the most intelligent of all hoofed animals, is probably descended from the wild boars that roamed Europe, Asia, and Africa more than 5,000 years ago. Wild boars still roam parts of Europe and Asia. A wild boar has two small tusks growing out of its lower jaw. The tusks can be very dangerous weapons. Pigs raised on farms usually get used to the presence of human beings, but wild boars are mean animals with vicious tempers.

Pigs are often called hogs or swine. A male pig is usually called a boar, and a female pig is called a sow. Pigs are cloven-hoofed animals with heavy, round bodies and short legs. Their skins are thick and partly covered with rough *bristles* (coarse hair). The pig has a long, flexible snout containing its nostrils and mouth, which has 44 teeth.

Pigs have been kept as domesticated animals since prehistoric times. Pigs are *omnivorous*, which means that they will eat anything that is vegetable or animal. When people discovered that pigs were easy to raise, they began to breed them in large numbers. Pork, ham, bacon, and spareribs all come from the meat of pigs. A pig's meat can be smoked or salted and can then be kept for a long time without spoiling. Lard, the fat of the pig, is used in cooking. Pig intestines are used as the casing for sausages. The pig's hide, when tanned, becomes the leather known as "pigskin," used to make such items as gloves and luggage. The stiff bristles from the pig's hide are made into paint brushes.

A sow gives birth to between 8 and 20 baby pigs at one time—two or three times a year. Pigs reproduce more rapidly and mature earlier than many other common meat-producing animals. Baby pigs are called piglets. A piglet weighs about

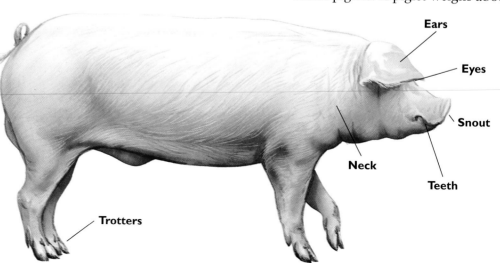

Ears

Eyes

Snout

Teeth

Neck

Trotters

▶ A diagram to show the different parts of a pig.

2½ pounds (1 kg) at birth, but gains weight quickly. When it is only one year old, a piglet can weigh 250 pounds (110 kg). The largest breeds may weigh as much as 600 pounds (270 kg) when they are full-grown.

Many different breeds of pigs have been developed in various parts of the world to meet local climate and pasture conditions. Eight separate breeds are widely raised in the United States. In modern farming practice, pigs are fed a carefully balanced diet containing proteins, carbohydrates, and minerals.

Like other animals, pigs are subject to a number of diseases—some of which are also dangerous to

Spotted swine

American landrace

Poland china

human beings who may eat the meat of infected animals. In the United States, the U.S. Department of Agriculture supervises and regulates the raising and processing of pigs throughout the country.

▶ ▶ ▶ ▶ **FIND OUT MORE** ◀ ◀ ◀ ◀
Food Processing; Mammal; Meat

PIGEON

Almost anywhere in the temperate or tropical parts of the world, you can find pigeons. You can see them in city streets and parks, in the country, and in the woods. Pigeons are medium-sized, stout birds. They have short, rounded beaks, topped by a fleshy part, called a *cere*, through which the nostrils open. Pigeons are very strong fliers. They strut when they walk, with their toes pointed slightly inward. People who walk with their toes pointed inward are said to be "pigeon-toed." Most birds tip their heads back after each sip when drinking. Pigeons, however, put their beaks in the water and pump the liquid down their throats, keeping their heads lowered. Some pigeons are called doves, but all belong to the same family of birds, the Columbidae.

A female pigeon lays two white eggs in a crudely built nest. Both parents take turns sitting on the eggs. The newly hatched pigeons cannot eat solid food. The parents feed them pigeon's milk. This is a liquid formed in the *crop* (a pouch in the throat) of the adult pigeon, and squeezed through the mouth into the throats of the pigeon chicks. Half-grown pigeons are called *squabs*. Some people raise pigeons for the squab meat.

Every part of the pig can be eaten or used for something. It has been said that the only useless part of the pig is its squeal.

◀ There are more than 53 million pigs on farms in the United States. About 20 breeds of pigs are raised, most of which were developed in the United States.

▼ Wood pigeons live in and around the deciduous forests of Eurasia. They make flimsy nests with twigs, and usually rear three broods in a year. Each brood normally consists of two chicks.

▶ City dwellers the world over know the urban pigeon. This bird is descended from the rock dove. It lives wild in towns and cities, feeding on whatever it can find, as well as on food provided by passersby.

Pigeons were the main source of fresh meat for the people of the Middle Ages.

▼ The mourning dove—named for its sad, cooing call—is a pigeon that is adapted to life in hot deserts. It needs little water and can withstand high temperatures.

There are more than 300 kinds of domestic and wild pigeons. The kind you see in parks and city streets is the common pigeon. The fantail pigeon can raise and spread its fanlike tail feathers. Most pigeons have 12 tail feathers, but the fantail has as many as 30. The tumbler pigeon turns somersaults as it flies. The homing pigeon can find its way back to its home from great distances. Homing pigeons have been used as message carriers, especially during wartime, and also as racing birds. Homing pigeons are sometimes taken several hundred miles from their home and then released. The pigeon that arrives home in the shortest time wins the race. The most common American wild pigeon is the mourning dove. It received its name from the mournful sound it makes. The largest pigeon is the goura, or crowned pigeon, of New Guinea, which is 3 feet (90 cm) long.

The passenger pigeon used to be very plentiful in the United States.

Once there were millions of them, but now they are extinct. Hunters killed so many of them through the years that now there are no passenger pigeons left. The last passenger pigeon died in the Cincinnati Zoo in 1914. Only 100 years before, John Audubon reported a flock of passenger pigeons so large that it took many hours for the flock to fly over him.

▶▶▶▶ FIND OUT MORE ◀◀◀◀
Audubon, John James; Bird; Birds of the Past

PIKE, ZEBULON (1779–1813)

Zebulon Pike was an American soldier and explorer. He was born in Lamberton (now part of Trenton), New Jersey, and entered the U.S. Army at the age of 15. In 1805, he was commissioned to lead a party to explore the upper regions of the Louisiana Purchase. He led the party into Minnesota, searching for the source of the Mississippi River. He mistakenly believed he had found it, but snow and ice covered the source. Pike bought land from the Sioux Native Americans to set up a fort near the point where

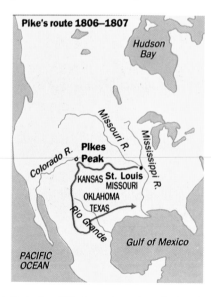

Pike's route 1806–1807

▲ Zebulon Pike's explorations helped to open the southwest of America.

the Minnesota River flows into the Mississippi River.

In 1806 and 1807, Pike led an expedition to explore Colorado and New Mexico. In central Colorado, he sighted a mountain that was later named Pike's Peak, but he did not succeed in climbing it. He followed the Arkansas River and Red River to their headwaters. On that expedition, he was arrested by Spanish soldiers in the city of Santa Fe and put in jail. After his release, he wrote an account of his travels.

Pike was a brigadier general during the War of 1812 against the British. On April 27, 1813, he was killed while leading a successful assault on York (now Toronto), Canada.

▶▶▶▶ **FIND OUT MORE** ◀◀◀◀
Colorado; Louisiana Purchase; Mississippi River; War of 1812

PILGRIM SETTLERS

The Pilgrim settlers were the group of English men and women who founded the first permanent European settlement in New England in 1620. Their settlement was Plymouth Colony (now Plymouth, Massachusetts). The Pilgrims sailed to America on a ship called the *Mayflower*.

Among the 102 settlers who sailed on the *Mayflower* were 35 members of a religious group called the English Separatist Church. The Separatists had broken away from the official Church of England, which they considered sinful and corrupt. They had been persecuted in England, and in 1608 and 1609, they fled to the city of Leiden in Holland. But most of the Separatists longed to find a place where they could farm the land and practice their religion in peace. William Brewster, one of the founders of the Separatist Church, obtained permission from the Virginia Company to start a settlement in America.

In July 1620, the Separatists sailed to Plymouth, England. They were joined there by other settlers. All the Pilgrims were crowded onto the *Mayflower*, and Brewster was made leader of the expedition. The voyage was stormy. Many people became ill, and some died. A son was born to Stephen and Elizabeth Hopkins and was named Oceanus. Strong winds forced the *Mayflower* to sail too far north. In November, the Pilgrims landed on Cape Cod. This area was not yet under the rule of any European country. The Pilgrims drew up the Mayflower Compact, under which they agreed to obey the laws made by their leaders.

After exploring a few miles of the coast of Massachusetts, the Pilgrims founded the settlement of Plymouth. A Separatist leader, John Carver, was elected governor. Carver guided the Pilgrims through their terrible first winter, when half the people died. In March 1621, Carver arranged a peace treaty with the Native American chief, Massasoit, who ruled the whole area of eastern Massachusetts. Carver died the following month. William Bradford succeeded him as governor.

The Native Americans taught the settlers how to grow crops, such as corn and squash. The autumn harvest was so plentiful that Governor

◀ The Pilgrim Fathers, who sailed from England in 1620, founded the first permanent European settlement in what is now Plymouth, Massachusetts.

Puritan settler

New England settler

New England farmer

The Pilgrims came mostly from East Anglia in eastern England. There is still a great deal in common between the speech of New Englanders and that of the people of East Anglia. There are many American English words that are no longer used in Britain, but many of these words would have been quite familiar to Shakespeare.

▲ A New England settlement. Between 1620 and 1700, about 400,000 people of European stock, most of them from England and France, were living in North America.

▲ A decorative Dutch ceramic tile depicting the Pilgrims' voyage of 1620. Due to religious conflict in England, many of the Pilgrims had first moved to Holland before they settled in North America.

Bradford invited Massasoit to a great feast—the first Thanksgiving celebration. Bradford was reelected governor almost every year until his death in 1657. Under his leadership, the colony grew larger and new settlements were founded. Bradford arranged for the people to hold town meetings. Each settlement sent representatives to a general council at Plymouth, which made laws for the colony. Bradford was assisted by Edward Winslow, who also served as governor for three years. Winslow had married Susanna White, the widowed mother of Peregrine White, the first child to be born in the Plymouth Colony.

Plymouth's small citizen army was trained by a professional soldier, Captain Miles Standish. He defended the colony several times against attacks by unfriendly Native Americans. A popular legend tells how Standish wanted to marry a young woman in Plymouth named Priscilla Mullens. Standish asked his friend John Alden to propose marriage for him. But Priscilla decided to marry Alden instead. John Alden served as an assistant governor of Plymouth.

The settlers were known for many years as the "Forefathers." But William Bradford, in his book *History of Plimoth Plantation*, had called them "pilgrimes." After this book was published in 1856, the settlers were named the Pilgrim Fathers.

▶▶▶▶ **FIND OUT MORE** ◀◀◀◀
Massasoit; Mayflower; Mayflower Compact; Thanksgiving

PIN

In primitive times, a long thorn or sharp fishbone was probably used as a pin to fasten clothing. Pins made of bronze were used in ancient Rome. The development of the wiremaking process led to the making of modern pins from brass, iron, and steel.

There are two main types of pins: straight, or common, pins and safety pins. Straight pins are used mostly in sewing. Safety pins, whose pointed ends slip into a protecting cap, are used mainly for pinning together clothing.

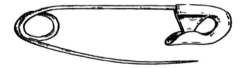

▲ A safety pin is very useful for holding clothing together.

PINE

SEE CONIFER

PIONEER LIFE

A territory yet to be explored is sometimes called a *frontier*. More than 200 years ago, pioneers moved into the unknown wilderness of North America where few people lived. As time passed, more and more people moved westward across the continent. The area once known as the frontier became settled. The settlers who moved there had to build their own houses, grow their own food, and attend to other needs themselves.

Frontier Houses

Most houses were built of logs, though some were made of clapboard overlapping wooden boards, and others were made of stone. In some parts of the West, where there

were few trees, families built houses of *sod* (grass-covered surface soil). Sometimes a group of families built log houses near a spring, and then built a log wall, or stockade, around the whole settlement as protection against Native American attacks.

Water had to be carried from lakes, rivers, or springs to the houses. In some areas, however, families dug wells near their homes. There was no plumbing in the early cabins.

Tables and benches were made of logs cut lengthwise. Legs were fastened to the curved side of a split log, and the flat side became the tabletop or the bench seat. Beds were often straw-filled mattresses on the cabin floor. Some settlers made wooden bed frames to which they tied ropes in crisscross fashion. The mattress rested on the rope network. Dishes and spoons were often made of wood, although some families brought pewter, silver, or china dishes with them when they moved West.

Family Life

The pioneer families had to make their own clothes. They hunted game for food and planted corn and other vegetables in their gardens. The Native Americans showed the first settlers what wild plants could be eaten or planted as crops.

Children had to help in housekeeping, gardening, taking care of the chickens and cows, and other chores. But they also found some time to play tag, blindman's buff, or other games. They also played with homemade dolls—some carved from wood, some made of rags. They climbed trees, ran races, went swimming, and fished in the local streams.

The settlers had to travel to the nearest town to get certain supplies, such as salt, sugar, and spices. These were needed to preserve or pickle meat and other foods. The people took furs, homemade whiskey, corn, or fruit to be traded for whatever they needed. The loads were carried on pack horses, and the journey often took several days.

Families usually went to bed as soon as it was dark, and they got up at sunrise. If they stayed up after dark, they used homemade candles

◄ When the first pioneers came to North America, they had to clear plots of land to build their settlements on. They often cleared woodland, and used the timber to build log cabins to live in.

▼ A pioneer family photographed in front of their sod house in South Dakota in 1882. By this date, pioneer settlers had more conveniences, such as glass windows, than those who had come earlier. Nevertheless, frontier life was still very tough for the pioneers.

to light the rooms. Later, after towns began to grow, they used kerosene lamps.

Few schools or churches existed in the first settlements. In many pioneer families, the father read from the Bible before meals or at bedtime. Traveling preachers on horseback, called *circuit riders*, sometimes visited frontier families and held prayer meetings and Bible readings in their homes. If there was no schoolhouse, children might be taught to read by their parents or by a neighbor.

Hardships of Frontier Life

Life on the frontier was lonely, and settlers occasionally visited neighbors who lived several miles away. Sometimes the hardworking farmers could enjoy being with other people at barn dances or picnics. Also, they all helped each other to build barns or other farm buildings. They joined with neighbors to help each other harvest crops, dig a well, or butcher hogs. If someone was sick or hurt, families used medicines or ointments made from the leaves and roots of plants and herbs they found, since few towns had a doctor.

Frontier life was very rough in both summer and winter. During summer dry spells, cows and other farm animals sometimes died from thirst and heat. Great armies of grasshoppers ate whole fields of wheat or other grain. The temperature often went down below freezing in the winter. The heat in many houses came only from the fireplace, and families often slept near the fire to keep warm. The cold weather, howling blizzards, and heavy snowstorms killed numerous cows and sheep.

The story of one pioneer family in Kansas tells of the terrible hardships they endured. This family brought with them everything they owned—a bed, a few chairs, a table, four horses, two oxen, some vegetable seeds, and a plow. During their first winter, their oxen and one horse froze to death. The following summer their vegetable garden was ruined for lack of rain. The man of the family said, "In God we trusted. In Kansas we busted."

Despite the hardships, the pioneers kept pushing westward. Villages and towns were settled all along the wagon trails. Gold was discovered in California in 1848, and thousands of people rushed to the gold fields. A coast-to-coast railroad was completed 21 years later, and the wild frontier was gradually tamed.

There are still many frontiers left in the world. Vast, wild areas in the interior of Australia are being explored and settled by pioneers from all over the world. Australia has fewer people than any other continent, except Antarctica, and the Australian government has encouraged people to settle there. Pioneers are also settling in previously uninhabited areas of Canada and in Siberia.

▶ ▶ ▶ ▶ **FIND OUT MORE** ◀ ◀ ◀ ◀
American History; Cowboy; Gold Rush; Oregon Trail; Railroad; Westward Movement

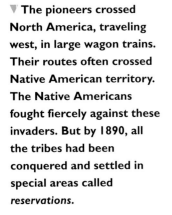

▼ **The pioneers crossed North America, traveling west, in large wagon trains. Their routes often crossed Native American territory. The Native Americans fought fiercely against these invaders. But by 1890, all the tribes had been conquered and settled in special areas called *reservations*.**

PIPELINE

The oil fields where petroleum and natural gas are found are often in distant deserts or under the sea bed. The oil and gas has to be brought to refineries for processing. Transportation of oil and gas is often done along a *pipeline*. Water and other liquids can also be sent along pipelines.

▲ The Alaskan pipeline snakes its way through scenic conifer forests below Mount Wrangell, which rises 14,163 feet (4,317 m).

Pipelines are large pipes that may be more than 3 feet (1 m) wide. They are made of steel and may be coated and lined with materials such as glass fiber and plastics to prevent corrosion. The pipes are often buried underground where they cross land. Pumps force the liquid or gas along the pipeline.

Some pipelines are very long. The Trans-Canada pipeline, which carries natural gas, is more than 6,000 miles (10,000 km) long. Another long pipeline is the Trans-Mediterranean pipeline, which carries gas from the Sahara Desert across the Mediterranean Sea to northern Italy. It is 1,500 miles (2,500 km) long. Under the sea, the pipe is covered in concrete to keep it from moving in the sea currents. In some places the pipeline spans undersea gulleys on steel supports.

Pipelines also carry materials such as coal, salt, chalk, and wood chips. These materials are forced through the pipe by moving water or air. Pipelines are also being built to carry bulky materials like grain in capsules, rather like small underground freight wagons.

▶▶▶▶ **FIND OUT MORE** ◀◀◀◀
Petroleum

PIRATES AND PRIVATEERS

A *pirate* is a robber on the high seas. Pirates recognize no government and obey no laws. In the past, a pirate captain divided the shares of treasure—money and other valuables—among the crew. *Privateers* were commissioned by their country's government to raid and capture the commercial ships of unfriendly or enemy countries. When privateers captured a prize, they shared the booty with the government they served.

As long as ships have carried goods across the ocean, there have been pirates. The Phoenicians, early navigators in the Mediterranean Sea, raided cargo ships. Vikings from Norway seized ships and raided villages along the coast of northern Europe. Arabs, called the Barbary pirates or corsairs, attacked and captured foreign ships along the Barbary

▼ During the period of colonization in the New World, many pirates preyed on ships and settlements in the Americas. The pirates would often take their stolen goods and cargoes to hideouts along the southeast coast of America.

Coast (North African coast on the Mediterranean Sea).

In the 1600s and 1700s, working conditions on merchant ships were poor. The food was bad, living quarters were crowded, and voyages were long. Sometimes sailors on merchant ships would rebel, or *mutiny*, against their captain and take over the ship. If this happened, the sailors could not go back to their home country or they would be thrown in jail. So they became pirates. Just before attacking a ship, they raised the pirate flag, the "Jolly Roger," with its white skull and crossbones on a black background.

The most active period for pirates was between the 1500s and the 1700s. Spanish trade ships then traveled between Spain and South and Central America. The ships were loaded with gold, jewels, and other booty from the lands the Spaniards had conquered. These treasure fleets attracted many pirates and privateers to the Caribbean Sea. The pirates who attacked Spanish ships off the mainland of South America (the Spanish Main) were known as *buccaneers*. They received this name from the *boucan*, or grill, they used for smoking and curing meat. They were also called *freebooters*.

One of the most famous buccaneers to attack these Spanish galleons was Henry Morgan. The British encouraged him to attack the Spanish. Morgan had a base at Port Royal, Jamaica. Port Royal was then called the most wicked city in the world. Warehouses there bulged with the gold and silver bars, silks, and jewels the pirates had taken. Morgan not only captured ships, he also raided coastal towns in

Venezuela and Panama. In a daring attack on Portobello, Panama, in 1668, Morgan and his 400 fighting buccaneers stormed and captured two well-defended forts. Then they seized the town itself. They held off a Spanish army force while Morgan obtained a ransom of 250,000 silver coins, silks, and 300 slaves.

English seamen and explorers such as Sir Francis Drake were also privateers. They raided Spanish ships with the full knowledge and blessing of the English queen, Elizabeth I. Captain William Kidd was a Scottish privateer. He wanted to be captain of a British man-of-war, but took charge of a *privateer* (the ship of privateers) instead. His ship roamed the Atlantic and

Indian oceans, capturing merchant ships and searching for pirates that preyed on British shipping. But Kidd did not turn over a fair share of the booty to the government. He was brought to trial in England, found guilty, and hanged.

► The pirate flag was known as the "Jolly Roger," and most commonly featured a white skull and crossbones on a black background.

► The English *buccaneer*, or pirate, Henry Morgan turned respectable citizen on the proceeds of his piracy. He became the deputy governor of Jamaica.

WHERE TO DISCOVER MORE

Fine, John Christopher. *Sunken Ships & Treasure.* New York: Atheneum Publications, 1986.

Schwartz, Alvin. *Gold & Silver, Silver & Gold.* New York: Farrar, Straus & Giroux, 1988.

One of the most feared pirates to operate in the Atlantic Ocean and Caribbean Sea was Blackbeard. His real name was Edward Teach. He was given the name Blackbeard because he had a long, black beard, which he wore in braids. Blackbeard attacked many defenseless merchant ships that sailed along the Carolina and Virginia coasts between 1716 and 1718. The southern planters grew furious as they lost their valuable cargoes. Finally a ship sent by the planters cornered Blackbeard off the coast of North Carolina. Blackbeard met his death fighting furiously with both sword and pistol.

Jean Laffite was a pirate who became an American patriot. He commanded a fleet of ships that put out from hidden coves along the Mississippi River delta. His group raided both Spanish and neutral ships in the Gulf of Mexico. Laffite offered his services to the United States during the War of 1812. He and his crew fought on the U.S. side against England. Laffite also helped General Andrew Jackson win the important Battle of New Orleans.

Later, Laffite went back to pirating. In 1821, the United States sent troops to destroy his pirate colony. Laffite saw that he would be overpowered, so he had his crew abandon and set fire to the pirate town. Then Laffite quietly sailed away. Historians do not know what finally became of him.

Sea piracy is now mostly a thing of the past. Careful patrolling by modern navies and improved communications between ships have made it almost impossible. However, pirates still make raids—particularly in the South China seas—preying on unarmed refugee boats and cargo ships. Since the 1970s, some travelers have experienced a modern form of piracy—airplane hijacking.

▶▶▶▶ **FIND OUT MORE** ◀◀◀◀
Drake, Sir Francis; Navy; Ships and Shipping; Spanish Main; Vikings

PISTOL

SEE GUNS AND RIFLES

PIZARRO, FRANCISCO (about 1478–1541)

After Christopher Columbus first came to America, Spanish *conquistadores*, or conquerors, sought gold and other wealth in South America. One of the most famous conquistadors was Francisco Pizarro.

Pizarro was born in Trujillo, Spain. His family was poor, and he never learned to read and write. He became a soldier and adventurer with no training for governing a colony. After sailing to the New World in 1510, Pizarro joined Vasco Núñez de Balboa's colony in what is now Panama. Pizarro was with Balboa when he crossed the Isthmus of Panama and saw the Pacific Ocean in 1513.

In 1532, a Spanish expedition led by Pizarro set out from Panama and sailed to Peru, where the Inca Indians had built a rich empire. The expedition landed on the coast of Peru at the time that two Inca rulers were quarreling over the throne. Pizarro and his soldiers captured and imprisoned Atahualpa, the Inca leader who had taken the throne. Pizarro received a huge treasure to free Atahualpa. But the Spaniards killed Atahualpa and many of his followers. Pizarro then seized the city of Cuzco (or Cusco), the great Inca capital.

After conquering the Inca Empire, Pizarro founded the city of Lima and called it the "City of Kings." He built a grand palace in Lima, now the capital of Peru. The Incas fought for years against their conquerors. In 1541, Pizarro was killed by the followers of his former partner, Diego de Almagro.

▶▶▶▶ **FIND OUT MORE** ◀◀◀◀
Balboa, Vasco Núñez de; Conquistador; Inca; Peru

Blackbeard, one of the fiercest pirates, carried six pistols into battle and fought with lighted matches framing his face. He scared friends by firing pistols under the table and lighting pots of sulfur. In his last fight, he suffered 25 wounds before he was shot dead. His head was put on a pole and shown to the Virginian settlers whom he had terrorized.

▼ The Spanish conqueror Francisco Pizarro. With only a few men, Pizarro managed to gain control of the Inca Empire.

▲ **Max Planck, the German scientist who totally changed physics. His quantum theory enabled scientists to answer important questions about the nature of energy.**

PLAGUE

SEE DISEASES

⚙ PLANCK, MAX (1858–1947)

The German physicist Max Karl Ernst Ludwig Planck is famous, because he was the first person to put forward the quantum theory of physics.

He was born in Kiel, Germany, and became professor of physics at Berlin University. He became interested in the way that objects behave when they are heated. If you have seen a piece of metal heated to a high temperature, you know that it becomes red-hot. Heated more, it becomes white-hot or even blue-hot. These different colors of light occur because the light being given off by the hot metal is of different wavelengths. The longer the wavelength, the less energy the light has. For example, red light has less energy than blue light and also has a longer wavelength.

Planck wondered why a hot object did not give off light of all colors. The only way that he could explain what really happens was to say that energy comes in small packages, or *quanta*. (The singular *quantum* is a Latin word meaning "how much.") The quantum is the smallest amount of energy that can exist; you cannot have half a quantum of energy.

Max Planck was awarded the Nobel Prize for physics in 1918.

▶▶▶▶ **FIND OUT MORE** ◀◀◀◀
Quantum

PLANET

SEE SOLAR SYSTEM

⚙ PLANETARIUM

A *planetarium* is a building inside which a special projector *projects* (shows) a picture of the sky onto a rounded ceiling. This projector works in much the same way a movie projector or a slide projector works, but is more complicated. A planetarium projector (also called a planetarium) is over 12 feet (4 m) high. It is shaped like a dumbbell, with a large metal *globe* (ball) at each end and an open framework that looks like a cage between them. Each globe contains 16 different slide projectors, and the middle framework contains several more slide projectors. The projectors in the globes show the stars, and those in the framework show the planets.

Inside a planetarium, you sit in a darkened, round room with a high, domed ceiling. In the middle of the room is the planetarium projector and an *astronomer* (a scientist who studies the stars and planets). When the projector is turned on, it seems as if you are outdoors on a clear night. The ceiling is covered with stars, so you seem to be gazing at the heavens.

In a planetarium, you can be shown about three times as many stars as you could see on the clearest night outdoors. The planetarium will show you stars that you could see only if you were on the other side of the Earth. One globe of the planetarium projector shows the northern sky (that part of the sky seen from north of the equator), and the other globe

▼ **The audience inside a planetarium can watch how the positions of the stars appear to change during the course of a year. The projector used can also show the tracks of the planets across the heavens.**

shows the southern sky. The projector turns to show how the sky looks from different places. In a planetarium, you can see how the sky would look from any place on the Earth, and even from places in outer space.

The planetarium can also speed up the movements of the stars and planets. In a few minutes, it can show all the movements of one night or one year. It can show you what the sky looked like on any day in history.

Many planetariums are controlled by a computer, but while the show is running, the astronomer explains what is happening in the sky and points out things you should notice. Planetariums often have special shows about imaginary trips through space.

The first planetarium was built by the Zeiss company in Germany in 1924, and the first planetarium in the United States opened in 1930. This was the Adler Planetarium in Chicago. Other large U.S. planetariums include the Fels Planetarium in Philadelphia, the Hayden Planetarium in New York, the Griffith Planetarium in Los Angeles, the Buhl Planetarium in Pittsburgh, the Morrison Planetarium in San Francisco, the East Lansing Planetarium in Michigan, the Charles Hayden Planetarium in Boston, and the Morehead Planetarium in Chapel Hill, North Carolina.

▶▶▶▶ **FIND OUT MORE** ◀◀◀◀
Astronomy; Constellation; Day and Night; Eclipse; Observatory

PLANKTON

SEE MARINE LIFE

PLANT

It is not hard to tell most plants from most animals. You can easily tell an oak tree from an ostrich or a rose

from a rabbit. But what exactly makes plants different from animals? First of all, most plants contain a green substance called *chlorophyll*. Chlorophyll enables them to make their own food. Almost all animals do not contain chlorophyll. Plants can take in only dissolved or liquid substances. Animals can eat both solids and liquids. Plant cells are surrounded by hard cell walls made of cellulose. Animal cells contain no cellulose. Most plants cannot move around under their own power, but most animals can.

Some plants have animal characteristics and vice versa. A few tiny, one-celled, plantlike animals contain chlorophyll, while plants such as mushrooms do not. The plants called slime molds can move from place to place under their own power during one part of their lives, and so can many minute water-living plants.

Where Plants Are Found

Plants live in nearly all parts of the world. Plants called *lichens* can grow in the extremely cold regions of the Arctic and Antarctic, and cacti grow in extremely hot deserts. Mushrooms can grow in dark caves, while algae can grow in the waters of seas, lakes, ponds, rivers, and streams. Plants are found at all levels of the land, from sea-level marshes to the peaks of high mountains. In the tropics, many kinds of plants grow in great numbers, because the hot, humid climate is good for plant growth. Plants live in many different environments. They have been able to adapt very well to almost all possible living conditions (climate, soil condition, and so on) found on Earth.

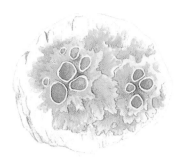

▲ A lichen is a simple plant that has no roots, leaves, or flowers. It grows very slowly, and often lives in places that are too bare, dry, cold, or hot for any other plant.

▲ There are hundreds of different cacti, all of which grow in hot desert climates. They are able to survive the heat because they store water in their fleshy stems.

▶ Mushrooms belong to the fungus group of plants. They feed on decayed matter.

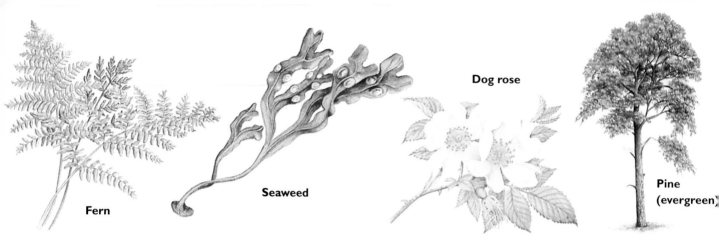

Fern

Seaweed

Dog rose

Pine
(evergreen)

▲ There are hundreds of different shapes and sizes of plants. Plants range from tiny specks you can see only under a microscope, to flowering species, to giant trees. In fact, there are more than 300,000 different kinds of plants. Plants grow in all sorts of environments—ferns like damp, shady places, and seaweeds, as their name suggests, live in the sea.

The fastest-growing plant is the bamboo. Some of these plants have grown 36 inches (91 cm) in a single day. Can you work out what speed this is in inches per hour?

▶ A typical plant cell. Inside the cell is a weak solution of salts and sugars. The *nucleus* is the cell's control center, the *chloroplasts* manufacture sugars and starches, and the *mitochondria* enable the plant to use its stored food by chemical processes.

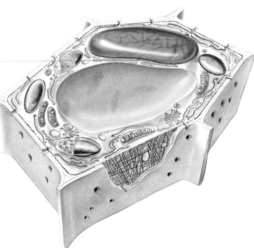

Kinds of Plants
Botanists, the scientists who study plants, have listed about 360,000 different kinds of plants. All plants together make up the *plant kingdom,* which is divided into four groups. The first group includes the simplest plants—*bacteria, algae, fungi,* and *lichens*—which have no stems, leaves, or roots. The second group, the *mosses* and *liverworts,* has parts resembling leaves, stems, and roots but lack food- and water-carrying tubes. The third group, the *ferns, club mosses,* and *horsetails,* has true leaves, stems, and roots, but lack seeds. The fourth group includes *seed plants*—cone-bearing trees (pines, firs, and so on) and flowering plants (grasses, roses, and so on).

Plant Structure
CELL. Every plant consists of one or more tiny cells. Large plants contain many millions of cells. Each cell is surrounded by a *cell membrane,* which all living things have. Outside this delicate membrane is a *cell wall,* which is found only in plants. Cell walls are made of *cellulose,* a hard, nonliving material. The cell wall protects the plant cell and helps it keep its shape. Cell walls give strength to plant tissues. The strength of cotton, for example, comes from the cellulose contained in its cell walls.

ROOTS. All plants must take in water. Algae take in water directly through the cell walls and cell membranes all over the plant surface. Mosses have no true roots but grow a network of long cells. These cells act much like roots because they take in water. The fern group and the seed plants have real roots that are used to take in substances from the soil.

Root systems consist of two main shapes. One has a single large root that grows straight downward with many tiny, thin roots growing out from it. Carrots and trees have this kind of root, which is called a *taproot.* The other root shape looks like a large number of strings, all growing downward and outward from the base of the stem. These are called *fibrous roots.*

One of the main jobs of the root is to take in water and minerals from the soil. At the thin ends of a root, there is a fuzzy growth called the *root hairs.* Each root hair is actually a single cell of the outer layer of the root. Growing roots have thousands of root hairs. Water and dissolved materials from soil pass through the walls and membranes of the root hairs. After water has entered a root hair, it is transferred from cell to cell toward the center of the root. From there, the water passes upward into the stem through long *xylem* tubes of cells, then outward to the branches and leaves. Another tube system, the *phloem*, carries food to the plant.

▼ A cross section of a root. Roots absorb water, minerals, and other substances from the soil they are in. These substances are carried around the plant and used for growth.

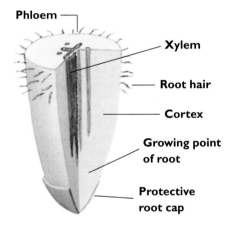

Another job of the root is to anchor a plant in the soil. The roots of large trees not only grow downward but also may grow more than a hundred feet outward from the tree. The roots must hold the tree upright against the force of strong winds.

Roots also store food. Sweet potatoes, radishes, carrots, and beets are roots in which plant food has been stored.

STEMS. The stem supports the leaves and flowers of a plant. Leaves may be attached directly to the stem, or they may be attached by short stalks. Some stems branch many times, and the leaves are attached to the smaller branches. Leaves of trees are attached to smaller branches or twigs.

The stem helps turn the leaves of a plant toward the light, without which the plant cannot make food. If you

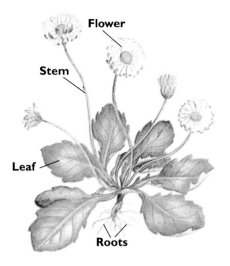

look at the leaves of a plant that has been sitting near a window, you will see the leaves are turned toward the sunlight. If you turn the plant around so that the leaves face away from the light, in two days the leaves will have turned back toward the light again. The movement of a plant in response to an outside force is called *tropism*.

Most plant stems store some food, usually only temporarily. However, some stems are the main storage area of the plant. The thick horizontal stems of the iris are storage stems. The main job of a stem is to conduct water and dissolved materials from the roots to the leaves, flowers, and fruit of the plant. Liquid food materials made in the leaves also move downward through the stem from the leaves to the roots. The liquid food material in the leaf stalk is called "sap."

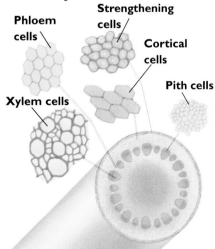

◀ The parts of a plant: The flowers are concerned with reproduction; the leaves are concerned with food making; the stem supports the leaves and flowers, and tubes inside it carry, and also store, food and water; roots anchor the plant in the soil, and they take in water and minerals through delicate hairs.

Some trees have long roots, with as much growth below the ground as above it. Others have massive trunks, but shallow roots.

◀ A cut-through stem of a flower reveals that plants have many different types of cells, arranged in groups in the stem, all performing specific tasks to help the plant grow.

▼ **The outer bark of a tree is a dead tissue that protects the living inner parts: the *phloem*, or inner bark, and the *xylem*, or inner wood.**

Bark

Phloem

Xylem

▼ **A cross section of a leaf. Plants depend on natural air (wind) to receive the carbon dioxide that they need to grow. Carbon dioxide passes in through holes, *stomata*, which are mainly on the undersides of the leaves.**

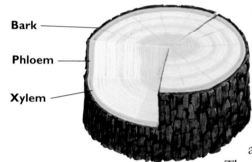

Upper leaf surface

Carbon dioxide passes through air spaces

Stoma

Carbon dioxide in

Lower leaf surface

Most stems grow above the surface of the ground, but some grow underground. The white potato is an underground stem that stores food.

Some stems, such as tree trunks, have a tough outer covering of dead cells that make up the outer bark. Just inside the inner bark is the *cambium* layer that causes the tree to grow in diameter. The cambium causes wood cells to form that carry water and minerals to the leaves. The cambium also makes tube cells for carrying food down the stem.

Celery and sunflowers are examples of *herbaceous* plants. They are not woody, although their stems may be quite tough. The cambium and conducting tubes, together with many tough fibers, form a ring in the stem.

LEAVES. Leaves are the food factories of a plant. Using water and carbon dioxide, the leaves make sugar. The leaves get energy for sugar making from sunlight. The green-colored substance of plants, called *chlorophyll*, causes the sugar-making process to take place. The chlorophyll absorbs the sun's light energy that is needed for the process to take place. This sugar-making process is called *photo-*synthesis. The sugar itself is used by the plant as food, or it may be converted to starches or oils for storage. The sugar is also used as the starting point for making cellulose and other materials, many of which are formed by combining the sugar with minerals obtained from the soil.

There are many kinds, shapes, and sizes of leaves. Tiny leaves, only one cell thick, are found on some kinds of mosses. Leaves of coconut palm trees may be 20 feet (6 m) long. The round, flat leaves of certain water lilies are more than 10 feet (3 m) across and can support small animals on the surface of the water. Leaves have many shapes. Some are round, others are long and thin. The needles of cone-bearing trees are leaves. Some leaves have smooth edges. Others are *serrated* (look like saw teeth). The broad, flat part of a leaf is called the *blade*. The stalk that holds the leaf to the stem is the *petiole*.

Leaves usually grow on a stem in certain patterns. Leaves may be opposite each other on the stem. Or they may grow in a circle around the stem. Leaves are arranged so that they do not shade each other all the time and can get as much light as possible.

Within a leaf are tubes to conduct food and water. These tubes are called *veins*. The veins are spread out in a network that leads to the petiole. Scattered all over the underside of a leaf are tiny openings called *stomata*. Carbon dioxide, which is needed in photosynthesis, enters through the stomata. The oxygen that is produced during photosynthesis is expelled through the stomata.

Plant Reproduction

One-celled plants reproduce by simple cell division. One cell divides into two cells, forming two new plants. Other plants, such as mushrooms and mosses, reproduce by forming tiny cells called *spores*. Each spore acts much like a seed. If it has good growing conditions, such as moisture and the proper temperature, the spore develops into a new plant.

The plants of the fern group grow from spores in two steps. First, the fern produces spores that grow into small plants that do not look like ferns. These plants produce male and female sex cells that unite and grow into a proper fern plant. This new plant then produces more spores.

Seed plants reproduce by means of male and female sex cells, in the process called *pollination*. In flowering plants, male sex organs, called *anthers*, produce *pollen*, which contains male sex cells. The pollen falls onto the female sex organ, called the *pistil*, which contains egg cells within *ovules*. Male cells from the pollen unite with egg cells to grow into *seeds*. Each seed contains a baby plant, called an *embryo*, and a supply of food, all enclosed in a tough coat. The seeds ripen and leave the plant. They may simply fall to the ground, or they may be carried long distances by wind, water, or on the coats of animals. When a seed falls in good soil that has the proper moisture and temperature, the embryo starts to grow and bursts out of the seed coat. It is then called a *seedling*. Some seedlings grow and scatter their own seeds in a few weeks, but trees take many years to mature. Each variety of plant has its own complete life cycle.

▶▶▶▶ **FIND OUT MORE** ◀◀◀◀

Kinds of Plants and Where They Grow see Algae; Bacteria; Cactus; Citrus Fruit; Club Moss; Conifer; Corn; Evergreen Tree; Fern; Flower Families; Fossil; Fungus; Garden Flowers; Grain; Grass; Horsetail; Houseplant; Insect-eating Plant; Lichen; Mosses and Liverworts; Mushroom; Orchid; Palm; Parasitic Plant; Petrified Forest; Plant Distribution; Plant Kingdom; Plants of the Past; Poisonous Plant; Rice; Rose; Shrub; Tree; Vegetables; Wheat; Yeast

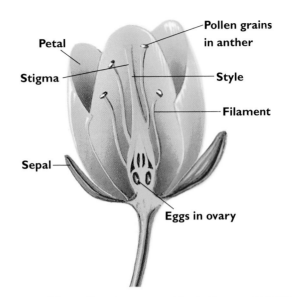

Petal — Stigma — Sepal — Pollen grains in anther — Style — Filament — Eggs in ovary

◀ **A cross section of a flower. In flowers that reproduce sexually, the male pollen is received at the stigma and moves down to the ovary, where it fertilizes the eggs.**

Plant Products see Alcoholic Beverage; Candy; Chocolate; Coal; Coffee; Cotton; Dye; Flour Making; Food; Furniture; Lumber and Lumbering; Natural Resources; Nut; Paint; Paper; Perfume; Petroleum; Plant Products; Plastic; Rubber; Sugar; Tea; Textile; Tobacco; Wines and Wine Making

Plant Structures and How They Work see Bulb; Cell; Fermentation; Flower; Fruit; Growth; Leaf; Photosynthesis; Regeneration; Reproduction; Respiration; Seeds and Fruit; Wood

Raising Plants see Agriculture; Botanical Garden; Conservation; Drought; Erosion; Fertilizer; Forestry; Gardening; Greenhouse; Irrigation; Plant Breeding; Plant Diseases; Soil; Truck Farming; Water

Sciences and Scientists Interested in Plants see Biology; Botany; Burbank, Luther; Carver, George Washington; Chemistry; Ecology; Linnaeus, Carolus; Nature Study

Most trees or plants receive only about 10 percent of their nutrition from the soil. The other 90 percent comes from the atmosphere.

PLANT BREEDING

Oranges without seeds and giant roses are plant products that were created by the science of *plant breeding*. This science breeds new plants

QUIZ

1. What are a plant's cell walls made of?
2. What do *xylem* do?
3. What are the four groups that make up the plant kingdom?
4. What is *tropism*?
5. Why are carrots and sweet potatoes known as "root" vegetables?

(Answers on page 2176)

▶ Plant breeders have developed varieties of strawberry plants that can produce large, juicy, disease-resistant fruit throughout the summer and the fall.

Cultivated strawberry plant

Wild strawberry plant

or changes the characteristics of existing plants.

Plant breeding began thousands of years ago when people noticed that certain plants gave better fruit than others of the same kind. The seeds from this fruit grew into plants that bore the better fruit.

Modern plant breeding is based on the laws of heredity discovered by Gregor Mendel. These laws enable plant breeders to predict what kinds of plants their breeding experiments will probably produce.

One of the most useful modern methods of plant breeding is *cross-pollination*. Pollen from one plant is placed on the pistil of another. The plants that result from cross-pollination are called crosses, or *hybrids*. By choosing the proper parent plants and planning the cross-pollination according to the laws of heredity,

plant breeders can produce hybrids that are either completely new or are stronger, larger, or better in some way.

Although breeders can often predict what might happen when they cross-pollinate plants under experimental conditions, growing plants from seed does not necessarily produce more plants just like the parents. With trees and shrubs it can also take a very long time for a seed to grow into a mature plant. Breeders who need lots of identical plants often take *cuttings* of small twigs or shoots that will take root in the soil and quickly grow into new plants just like the original ones.

Another method, much used by fruit growers, is *grafting*. A live twig or bud from one kind of tree is attached to the live stump of another tree. The twig or bud is called a *scion*, and the tree it is attached to is the *stock*. The stock provides roots for the scion. The trunk and branches that eventually grow from the scion have the characteristics of the scion. For example, an apple grower may find a tree that has bigger or tastier apples than those on other trees. He or she cuts twigs with sturdy buds from the tree, and grafts the twigs to stocks of other apple trees. The apples that grow from the scions will be the same as those that grew on the tree from which the scion was cut.

▼ Grafting a twig from one apple tree onto another. If the twigs are cut carefully as shown, then bound tightly together, they will grow together. In this way it is possible to grow two kinds of apples on one tree.

▶▶▶▶ **FIND OUT MORE** ◀◀◀◀
Agriculture; Burbank, Luther; Genetics; Mendel, Gregor; Plant

PLANT DISEASES

Plants, as well as animals, suffer from disease. Scientists have not yet found a plant that is completely immune to disease. Plant diseases are caused by several kinds of parasites and by poor soil conditions. Plant diseases damage many millions of dollars worth of crops each year.

Dryad's saddle fungus

The most serious plant parasites are *fungi*. Next come *viruses*, and then *bacteria*. Fungi and bacteria are themselves plants. One-celled animals and microscopically small worms are other parasites that cause plant diseases.

Hundreds of different types of fungi live on plants. The harmful fungi are *rusts*, *smuts*, and *mildews*. Viruses live within the cells of the plants they attack. Bacteria usually occupy the spaces between the cells of a plant's tissues. These parasites cause a wide range of tumors, warts, and leaf spots. They may also cause the plants to wilt and various parts to rot away. They can stunt a plant's growth, causing it to be dwarfed.

High temperature, high humidity, and lack of sunlight favor the development of plant diseases. The parasites are carried from plant to plant by wind, rain, birds, insects, and people. Packing a few unhealthy fruits, vegetables, or grains along with healthy ones is another way of spreading plant diseases. Shipping diseased crops over long distances may spread a plant disease throughout a whole country.

◄ **A potato plant with leaf roll virus. This disease makes the leaves so brittle that they rattle if the plant is shaken.**

Plant diseases caused by parasites can be fought by spraying crops with chemicals that kill the parasites. Another way is to breed plants that resist parasite infection. A third way to stop plant disease spreading is to prevent plants from being shipped or taken out of an area in which a plant disease is raging. This is usually done by inspecting or stopping crop shipments at the borders of states or countries.

Plants suffer disease due to poor conditions in the environment that they grow in. The soil may have too much acid or too much alkali. It may contain too much or too little of the chemicals that plants need for healthy growth. Poor soil harms plants just as poor diets harm human beings. Plants often die from struggling to grow in poor soil. Severe air and water pollution kills plants or weakens them so much that they become infected very easily by diseases.

► ► ► ► **FIND OUT MORE** ◄ ◄ ◄ ◄
Air Pollution; Bacteria; Disease; Ecology; Fungus; Parasitic Plant; Plant; Soil; Virus; Water Pollution

◄ **Fungi are parasites. They cannot make their own food, so they take it from other plants. In the process, the host plant suffers loss of its own nutrition and may develop diseases.**

PLANT DISTRIBUTION

Different kinds of plants grow in different places. Willows grow along the banks of streams. Cattails grow in swamps and marshes. Sunflowers grow in fairly dry areas with lots of

Plants can be found almost everywhere on earth. Divers found seaweed growing at a depth of 880 feet (270 m) off the coast of the Bahamas. At that depth there is almost total darkness.

VEGETATION ZONES OF THE EARTH

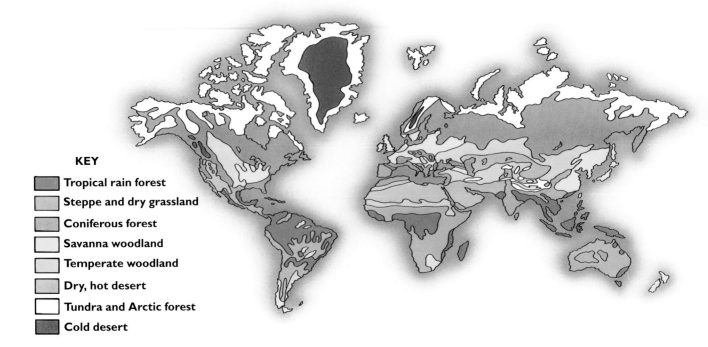

KEY

■ Tropical rain forest
□ Steppe and dry grassland
■ Coniferous forest
□ Savanna woodland
□ Temperate woodland
■ Dry, hot desert
□ Tundra and Arctic forest
■ Cold desert

▲ This map shows the main vegetation zones of the world. Climate, soil, altitude, and the effect of people and animals are factors that determine plant distribution.

▼ Plants that live in hot deserts have adapted to their environment for their own survival. Many of them have spiny leaves and fleshy stems for storing water. They flower quickly after a rainfall.

sunshine. Cacti grow in extremely hot and dry desert areas. Every plant is adapted for life in a certain kind of environment, and if it is not adapted for a particular place, it cannot live there. This is what plant distribution is all about. Maple trees, for example, need a certain amount of water in order to survive. A desert has hardly any water, so a maple tree will die if it is planted in a desert environment. Similarly, palm trees and cacti cannot grow in the cold climate of Alaska. The giant redwood trees of northern California are unable to grow in Florida because there is not enough rain.

Plant Environment

All plants are dependent upon a particular environment, which includes the climate, moisture, and soil type of the area, as well as other plants and animals that live there.

CLIMATE. The temperature in an area affects how fast a plant can take in food. Low temperatures slow down a plant's ability to take in food. In very cold northern areas, the ground is frozen during many months of the year. A plant needs water, but it cannot take in ice through its roots, nor can it dissolve the nutrients in frozen soil. Trees in cold environments have adapted by storing food in their trunks. The sap of evergreen trees and maples is an example of this food storage.

The amount of rainfall is another factor that determines plant distribution. Only part of a rainfall reaches a plant's roots. The rest runs off into streams or evaporates. Sometimes the water goes down too far into the soil so that plants with shallow roots cannot reach it. In rain forests, where there is a great deal of water and heat, plants grow very rapidly and reach very large sizes. Desert areas are hot and have very little rainfall. Plants living there must protect themselves from water evaporation and get as much moisture from the soil as possible. Cactus plants are shaped so that any rain falling on them immediately runs down to the ground to be absorbed by the roots. Cactus plants also have needlelike leaves. Raindrops do not cling to them and evaporate, as on larger-leafed plants.

The rain quickly falls off the needles to the ground, where the roots absorb it.

Sunlight is necessary for *photosynthesis* (a food-making process) to take place. All green plants need sunlight. But green plants that live in areas of little sunlight have developed adaptations to make food manufacturing faster and more efficient. Ferns, for example, grow on the floors of dense forests where very little light filters through the taller trees and shrubs. Ferns have developed broad leaves, called *fronds*, that fan out over a large area to capture as much available sunlight as possible.

Humidity is the amount of moisture in the air. High humidity keeps moisture in the soil from evaporating. Desert areas have little humidity, and evaporation takes place very quickly. Rain forests have the highest humidity. The soil stays moist all the time, and plants grow to very large sizes.

Wind causes a high rate of evaporation. Plants living in windy environments have to be able to absorb water quickly. They must also cut down the rate of evaporation from their leaves. Many mountain-living plants do this by means of a hairy covering on their leaves. Strong winds can also uproot plants. In seacoast areas that have heavy winds, plants are short, or dwarfed. Their roots are spread out over a wide area in order to get water quickly and to hold the plant to the ground.

SOIL. Plants obtain water and nutrients from the soil. Sandy soil does not hold water for very long. Plants such as dune grass are adapted to sandy conditions. They have root systems that spread out in all directions to get water quickly as it filters through the sand. Clay soils hold water for long periods of time.

Soils vary in the amount and kinds of nutrients they contain. Plants that need a certain kind of nutrient, such as *phosphorus*, will grow best in soil that contains a great deal of it.

MAIN PLANT ENVIRONMENTS OF THE WORLD

Tundra

Short, cool summers with very long days of continuous light. Soil frozen most of the year, but thaws down about 2 feet (61 cm) in summer.
Main plants: grasses, dwarf shrubs, lichens, and mosses.

Coniferous Forest

Short, cool summers, but warmer than in tundra region. Long, cold winters with much snow. Soil completely thawed in summer.
Main plants: cone-bearing evergreen trees (spruces, firs, birches, and pines) and deciduous larches.

Deciduous Forest

Winters and summers about equal in length. Mild to fair temperatures. Soil rarely frozen. Medium rainfall. Great variety of plants.
Main plants: deciduous trees (those that lose leaves in the fall) and shrubs, with a carpet of small flowering plants.

Grassland

Evenly mild temperatures with seasonal variations and medium rainfall. Wide-open, flat, or rolling landscape.
Main plants: grasses with deciduous trees along edges of water bodies.

Desert

High temperatures, low rainfall, fast evaporation. Little plant cover. Soil dry and usually sandy.
Main plants: succulent species such as cacti, drought-resistant shrubs such as sagebrush and yucca trees, with a few short-blooming desert flowers after rainfall.

Tropical Rain Forest

High temperatures, high humidity, much rainfall. Heavy, very tall plant cover. Soil always moist.
Main plants: flowering evergreen trees, including palms, climbing vines, and aerial plants perched on the branches of the trees.

Aquatic Regions

Wide range of temperatures in bodies of fresh and salt water. Great variety of water plants.
Main plants: algae, duckweeds, sedges, and water lilies in ponds, lakes, and rivers; brown and red algae (seaweed) and eelgrass in oceans, mainly around the coasts.

▲ **Tropical forests contain half the known plant species. Most tropical forest trees are evergreen trees.**

The biggest cactus is the saguaro of Arizona and Mexico. It has branches that grow to a height of 52 feet (16 m), about nine times the height of a man. Large saguaro cacti may weigh as much as two elephants. Three-fourths of this weight is in the water they store in their great stems.

OTHER PLANTS AND ANIMALS. A plant's survival depends on the other forms of life around it. In a garden environment, for example, weeds can use up the soil nutrients and water that were meant for flowers or vegetable crops. Plant parasites attack plants and feed off them, either killing the plants or making them unable to produce seeds. The chestnut blight and Dutch elm parasites have destroyed whole families of trees in the United States.

Grazing animals feed on grasses. The droppings from these animals provide fertilizer that enriches the soil and helps plants grow. Squirrels store food by burying nuts, such as acorns. The squirrel never eats all the acorns it buries, and so the buried acorns grow into oak trees.

People cultivate many crops, cut down many trees, and dig up the land to build highways and buildings. All these activities change the distribution of plants. People also

in order to save plants from ruin or extinction. People have built greenhouses so plants from warmer regions can be grown in colder areas of the world. All of these things affect plant distribution.

FIRE. Uncontrolled fire is probably the worst enemy of plants. A very big forest fire can totally destroy all the plants in an area. The giant sequoias and redwood trees grow only in a small area on the West Coast of the United States. It takes thousands of years for one sequoia to reach its full height. One fire could destroy all the sequoia trees forever. Forest rangers and fire wardens constantly watch for the smallest signs of fire both in forest and grassland areas. On the other hand, not all fire is bad. Foresters often use controlled fire to burn off forest undergrowth that has become too heavy and thick.

Barriers

Plant distribution is also affected by natural formations, such as oceans, high mountains, and wide deserts. These *barriers* keep the seeds of plants in one area from spreading to another area. So conditions may be alike in two areas, but the plants they support may be different. Seeds that grow on an island in the middle of the ocean would have a hard time reaching the mainland. In Hawaii, three-fourths of the plants growing there do not grow in other parts of the world.

Temperature can also be a barrier. Plants that grow at the base of a tall,

▼ Typical plants of the cool temperate woodland include deciduous trees such as beech, oak, and maple and a variety of woodland flowers such as bluebells.

weaken and kill many plants with air and water pollution, as well as poor farming methods that reduce the nutrients in the soil. Much *soil erosion* (washing away of soil) and other loss of soil is caused by strip mining. However, people are experimenting with plant breeding in order to create better kinds of vegetables, flowers, and trees. They are studying ecology to find out how plants and other forms of life are affected by changes in the environment. They are practicing conservation methods

▶ A variety of plants such as lilies, reeds, and willow and mangrove trees, flourish in wetland areas. Some of the wetland plants live completely under water, while others live on the surface with their roots submerged in the water.

snowcapped mountain cannot survive the cold temperatures at the top. Seeds that may get blown to the top will not grow there. Very tall mountains have what is called a *timberline*. The timberline marks the greatest height at which trees are able to grow without freezing.

Some of these natural barriers have been overcome. The potato used to be found only in the Andes Mountains of Peru. In the 1500s, Spanish explorers brought potato plants back to Europe. Now, the potato grows in almost every cool climate.

▶▶▶▶ **FIND OUT MORE** ◀◀◀◀

Air Pollution; Cactus; Climate; Conservation; Desert; Ecology; Erosion; Fern; Forest Fire; Humidity; Jungle; Parasitic Plant; Photosynthesis; Plant; Prairie; Rain and Snow; Soil; Tree; Tundra; Water Pollution

PLANT KINGDOM

All of the plants on Earth are members of the plant kingdom. In order to keep track of them all, botanists divide the plant kingdom into groups. The plants in each group are all alike in some way. Each large group is called a *division*. The members of a division are alike only in a few very general ways. A division includes thousands of kinds of plants that may look very different from each other. For instance, pond scum and mushrooms are members of the same division. A division is divided into smaller groups called *classes*. The

classes are divided into *orders*, and the orders are divided into *families*. Families may still include a large number of members. The daisy family, for example, has 20,000 members. The next group smaller than a family is a *genus*, and the members of a genus are called *species*.

Some Plant Divisions

THALLOPHYTES are simple flowerless plants without roots, stems, or leaves. They may have only one cell or millions of cells. The thallophyte division includes *algae, bacteria*, and *lichens*.

Algae contain chlorophyll, which means that they are green plants, although the green color may be hidden by other pigments. Algae vary from single-celled, microscopically small species to many-celled seaweeds up to 200 feet (60 m) long.

At one time, fungi, such as mushrooms and molds, were classified only as thallophytes. Today, fungi are regarded as a separate Kingdom.

Fungi do not contain chlorophyll. This means that fungi do not make their own food and so do not need sunlight in order to grow. They get their food either by living on other plants as parasites, or by living on the decaying remains of dead plants and animals.

BRYOPHYTES are *mosses* and mosslike plants. Mosses are small, green, flowerless plants. Like all bryophytes, mosses have no real roots, just fine hairs that absorb water from the soil. They are sometimes found on walls. Many *liverworts* are flat, branching bryophytes resembling green seaweeds, although they live on land. Other liverworts are like mosses, and are among the simplest of all land plants.

PTERIDOPHYTES are complex plants that have true roots, stems, and leaves, but no flowers or seeds. Ferns are the main type of pteridophyte. Other pteridophytes include *club mosses* and *horsetails*.

◀**Alpine plants and flowers survive the wind and cold on high mountains by growing near to the ground and having long clinging roots.**

▲ **The pine is an evergreen conifer tree, and its seeds are carried in cones. It is a gymnosperm—part of the spermatophytes division of the plant kingdom.**

RECORD TREES

Tallest are the California-coast redwoods, which grow over 300 feet (91 m) high.

Thickest trunk is that of a Montezuma cypress in Mexico, with a diameter of 40 feet (12 m).

Oldest are the bristlecone pines of Nevada, California, and Arizona—nearly 5,000 years old.

Longest surviving species is the maidenhair tree, or ginkgo, of China; it first appeared about 160 million years ago.

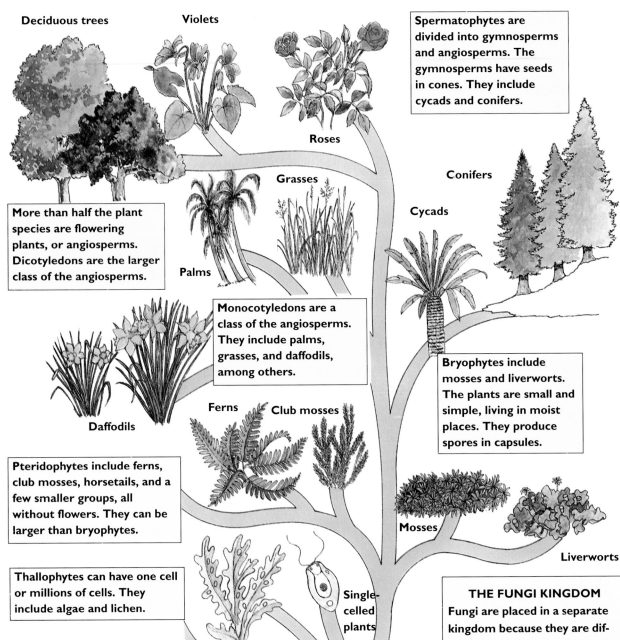

Deciduous trees

Violets

Roses

Spermatophytes are divided into gymnosperms and angiosperms. The gymnosperms have seeds in cones. They include cycads and conifers.

Conifers

Grasses

Cycads

More than half the plant species are flowering plants, or angiosperms. Dicotyledons are the larger class of the angiosperms.

Palms

Monocotyledons are a class of the angiosperms. They include palms, grasses, and daffodils, among others.

Bryophytes include mosses and liverworts. The plants are small and simple, living in moist places. They produce spores in capsules.

Daffodils

Ferns

Club mosses

Pteridophytes include ferns, club mosses, horsetails, and a few smaller groups, all without flowers. They can be larger than bryophytes.

Mosses

Liverworts

Thallophytes can have one cell or millions of cells. They include algae and lichen.

Single-celled plants

Algae

THE PLANT KINGDOM

Several systems are used to classify the 450,000 or so kinds of plants that belong to the plant kingdom. The main divisions, or phyla, of the plant kingdom are the Thallophyta, Bryophyta, Pteriodophyta, and the Spermatophyta. The spermatophytes make up the largest phylum, consisting of more than 350,000 different species, which reproduce by way of seeds. There are two kinds of seed-bearing plants, the *gymnosperms*, or naked seed plants, and the *angiosperms*, or covered seed plants. The angiosperms, which include all of the flowering plants, are divided into two classes, the monocotyledons, plants with one seed leaf, and the dicotyledons, plants with two seed leaves. The other phyla do not produce flowers and all reproduce by scattering particles, which are called spores.

THE FUNGI KINGDOM

Fungi are placed in a separate kingdom because they are different from plants and animals. They include toadstools, yeasts, and molds. They live almost anywhere in the soil, water, and air. They do not produce their own food, since they have no chlorophyll, so they take nutrients from the animals, plants, or decaying matter on which they live. They reproduce by spores—sexually or asexually.

SPERMATOPHYTES are the true seed plants. They also have roots, stems, and leaves. They include all flowering plants. Seed plants replaced most of the other types of plants that existed in the past. This means that seed plants have been the most successful in adapting to climate and soil conditions that exist on Earth today.

There are two kinds of spermatophytes: *gymnosperms* and *angiosperms*. The gymnosperms, or naked seed plants, include the *coniferous* (cone-bearing) trees and shrubs. Within the cones, the seeds of the plant lie exposed and unprotected. Pines, firs, spruces, hemlocks, and junipers are all gymnosperms; as are the largest plants on Earth, the redwood trees. The leaves of many gymnosperms are in the form of needles, which remain on the plant all year round. This is why the trees are called evergreens.

Angiosperms, or covered seed plants, include such different plants as grasses, maple trees, roses, and orchids. The seeds of these plants are protected with a fruit. There are more than 200,000 species of angiosperms—more than half the number of all known plants.

The angiosperms are divided into two classes: *monocotyledons* and *dicotyledons*. The seeds of monocotyledons contain a single seed leaf, or *cotyledon*. Grasses, including grains such as wheat, buckwheat, and rye, are monocotyledons. So are bananas, onions, coconut palms, and orchids.

The seeds of dicotyledons have two seed leaves. There are nearly five times as many dicotyledons as there are monocotyledons. Dicotyledons are the best of all plants at adapting to different environments.

PLANT PRODUCTS

A very large number of products that are useful to human beings are produced from plants—more than from any other source.

Food is the most important product that comes from plants. There are cereals such as wheat, rye, barley, and corn. There are dozens of fruits—apples, pears, peaches, cherries, grapes, and so on. Berries and nuts, such as raspberries, blackberries, strawberries, peanuts, walnuts, and cashews, all come from plants. Vegetables, such as potatoes, tomatoes, peas, beans, celery, broccoli, lettuce, and onions, all come from plants. Spices, such as pepper, cinnamon, cloves, mustard, and ginger, are also plant products. Sugar comes from sugarcane, a member of the grass family, and from sugar beets, which are similar to regular garden beets. Coffee, tea, and hot chocolate are three popular beverages that are made from plants. Soybean is one of the main ingredients in such different products as margarine and plastics. Grasses and other plants are

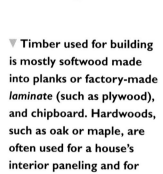

▼ All animals depend on plants for their food in some way. The most important food crops grown by people include wheat, maize, rice, potatoes, beans, cassava, fruits, and vegetables.

▼ Timber used for building is mostly softwood made into planks or factory-made *laminate* (such as plywood), and chipboard. Hardwoods, such as oak or maple, are often used for a house's interior paneling and for finished floors.

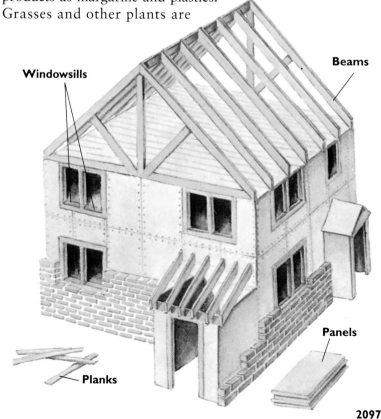

Windowsills

Beams

Panels

Planks

▲ Reeds are bound together to make these simple boats used on Lake Titicaca in the Andes Mountains of South America.

▼ Many different parts of plants can be used to make other products. The sap of the rubber tree is tapped to give latex, which is used to make natural rubber. Cotton comes from the ripe fruit of the cotton plant. Cork comes from the bark of the Mediterranean cork oak; the cork is stripped from the tree once every nine or ten years.

also very important as food for cattle and other livestock.

The most widely used building material—wood—comes from trees, which are plants. Houses of wood have been built in every part of the world. Stone, brick, earth, or baked mud houses usually have roofs, inside walls, stairs, window sashes, and other parts made of wood. In tropical countries, walls and roofs of houses may be made of coconut or banana leaves. Roofs of houses are also made of *thatch*—straw or twigs woven together. Wood logs are used to make jetties, wharves, docks, and telephone poles. Wood is still a favorite material for making boats. Most furniture is made of wood.

Tables, chairs, desks, beds, bureaus, and cabinets may be made entirely or partly of wood. However, the commercial destruction of millions of trees, particularly in tropical rain forests, is causing growing environmental concerns.

Tobacco is the leaf of a plant that is smoked in pipes, cigars, and cigarettes. Plant leaves are also the source of indigo and other dyes used for coloring cloth. The bark of many trees produces *tannin*, a substance used in tanning leather to make it soft as well as long-wearing.

Plants provide fibers that are made into cloth. Cotton and flax fibers are spun into thread, and the thread is woven into cloth. Clothing, curtains, furniture coverings, and hundreds of other products are made from cloth. The raw material for the artificial fiber rayon is *cellulose*, which comes from plants. Rope is made from hemp fibers. Fibers of the jute plant are woven into burlap sacks and made into twine.

Paper is made from wood or linen (which comes from flax). Paper is used for writing, printing, or wrapping. It is made into bags, boxes, dishes, and many other products.

Certain trees secrete gums and resins that harden in the air into

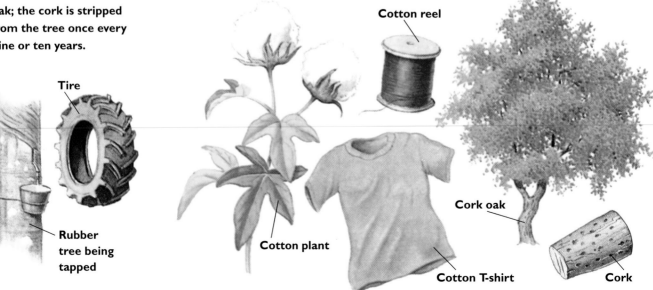

Tire

Rubber tree being tapped

Cotton plant

Cotton reel

Cotton T-shirt

Cork oak

Cork

sticky or stiff masses. Gums and resins have many uses. Gum arabic, which comes from acacia trees, is used in inks, glues, candies, and medicines. Rubber is made from a gum called latex that comes from the rubber tree. Pine trees give off a mixture of gum and resin that is made into turpentine, which is used in paints. Pine resin is used in the making of soap, sealing wax, varnish, lacquer, and paint. *Chicle* (the sap of a tropical evergreen tree, the *sapodilla*) is the main ingredient of chewing gum.

Except for nuclear fuel, all fuels are plant products. Wood is still burned as fuel in many parts of the world. Coal, lignite, and peat are fossilized plants that are burned as fuel. Oil comes from petroleum, which is partly the decayed and fossilized remains of blue-green algae.

◄ The flower of the cinchona tree, from which *quinine* (used to treat malaria) is made.

Many plants are used as medicines or the sources of medicines. Quinine, once used to combat malaria, comes from the bark of the cinchona tree. Digitalis, a medication for heart disease, comes from the foxglove. Ephedrine, used to relieve hay fever, comes from evergreen trees.

▶▶▶▶ **FIND OUT MORE** ◄◄◄◄
Alcoholic Beverage; Building Material; Candy; Chocolate; Coal; Coffee; Cotton; Dye; Flour Making; Food; Furniture; Lumber and Lumbering; Natural Resources; Nut; Paint; Paper; Perfume; Petroleum; Plant; Plastic; Rubber; Sugar; Tea; Textile

PLANTS OF THE PAST

Scientists believe that plants were the first living things. The oldest known fossils are remains of single-celled plants much like the single-celled blue-green algae plants of today. The rocks in which these fossils were found are thought to be nearly three billion years old.

For the first $1\frac{1}{2}$ billion years of life on Earth, many scientists believe that all living things lived in the ocean. The first plants were various kinds of bacteria and *algae*. Some single-celled algae became many-celled. These primitive plants resembled the seaweeds that live today in the ocean. Even primitive algae contained *chlorophyll*, the green substance that enables plants to make their own food using sunlight. The first algae must have lived near the surface of the water in order to get the needed sunlight. For many millions of years, they were the only living things on Earth.

After a time, plants like algae, but without chlorophyll, appeared. To get food, they had to live on other algae that were either alive or dead and decaying. These new plants were the first *fungi*. But because there are very few fossil fungi, botanists don't really know how they arose.

The Land Plants
About 420 million years ago, many scientists think that plants began to live on land. Among the first was a plant called *Cooksonia*; It was a leafless stalk just a few inches tall. The upper end branched, and on the branches were small pods. These held *spores*, the cells from which new Cooksonia plants grew. Another kind of early land plant was the *lichen*. A lichen is really two plants living together—an alga and a fungus.

The oldest plant fossil was found near Victoria, Australia, in 1989. It looks like a modern green pepper and is thought to be 120 million years old.

▲ The hardened fossil remains of a fern formed in a coal seam underground.

▲ Fossil remains of a small horsetail named *Spenophyllum*.

▲ A fossil of *Lepidodendron*, the largest of all the club mosses, which could grow to a height of about 100 feet (30 m). Some specimens may have been 130 feet (40 m).

▶ **This is what a swamp forest was like 300 million years ago. Giant horsetails and club mosses grew as tall as modern trees. Many fossil remains of leaves and stems of mosses and horsetails have been found.**

▲ **The fossil remains of a giant horsetail called *calamites*. This horsetail grew to a height of about 60 feet (18 m).**

The earliest land plants lived in mud at the shoreline of the ocean, because there was no soil farther inland. The land was bare rock covered by rock dust that had been building up for millions of years. Some of this windblown dust piled up around the plants along the shore. When they died, their decaying remains mixed with the rock dust. This formed the first soil. Spores grew in the soil, and the plants that grew from them formed more soil when they died. It took about 100 million years from the time of the first land plants for most of the land to become covered with soil and plants.

As soil spread over the land, plants were able to grow bigger and bigger. There were tree-ferns 100 feet (30 m) tall and horsetails 60 feet (18 m) tall.

THE COAL FORESTS. About 340 million years ago, many scientists believe that the climate all over the Earth was tropical. It remained warm for about 60 million years. The land was often flooded by the ocean, forming vast, swampy areas. In this warm, moist climate, plants grew abundantly. Besides tree-ferns and horsetails, there were *calamites*. These were related to the horsetails, but grew to be 100 feet (30 m) tall and had whorls of flat or needlelike leaves. There were *scale trees,* whose trunks had scalelike scars where leaves had dropped off. *Seal trees* had seal-like scars where leaves had dropped off. About this time, *Cardaites* appeared. These were the first *conifers,* or cone-bearing trees—the ancestors of modern conifers.

All these plants grew quickly to gigantic sizes, died, and fell into the swamps. Layer upon layer of dead plants piled up and sank deep into the mud. The covering of mud kept them from decaying. The pressure of their own weight, together with pressure and heat from movement of the Earth's crust, slowly changed the deeply buried trees into coal.

SEED FERNS AND CONIFERS. Ferns reproduce by means of spores, but some early kinds of ferns bore seeds instead of spores. These seed ferns were the ancestors of the conifers. Seeds grew within the cones of the conifers. Plants that bore seeds that were protected in fruits probably also developed from these original seed ferns.

CYCADS AND GINKGOES. Many scientists believe that about 250 million years ago, when the Earth was in one of its warm periods, there was a kind of tree that resembled a palm, with a very thick, rough trunk. This was the *cycad.* Cycad trees spread widely over the Earth, and then almost died out. Today, about 100 kinds of cycads grow in tropical areas, including Mexico and

South America. From the conifers there came *Ginkgo* trees. These, too, spread widely, and then almost died out. Today, the maidenhair trees of Asia are the last of the ginkgoes.

Cereals, Fruits, and Grasses

By about 65 million years ago, most of the kinds of plants living today had appeared. There were grasses, including wheat and rye, and flowering herbs, as well as fruit and nut trees. One 63-million-year-old rock contains the fossilized leaves of such well-known plants as pepper, alder, and walnut.

▶ ▶ ▶ ▶ **FIND OUT MORE** ◀ ◀ ◀ ◀

Algae; Bacteria; Coal; Earth History; Evergreen Tree; Evolution; Fern; Flower; Fossil; Fungus; Grass; Horsetail; Lichen; Marine Life; Ocean; Petrified Forest; Photosynthesis; Plant; Plant Distribution; Plant Kingdom; Seeds and Fruit; Soil

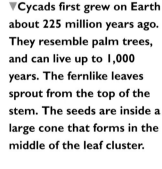

▼Cycads first grew on Earth about 225 million years ago. They resemble palm trees, and can live up to 1,000 years. The fernlike leaves sprout from the top of the stem. The seeds are inside a large cone that forms in the middle of the leaf cluster.

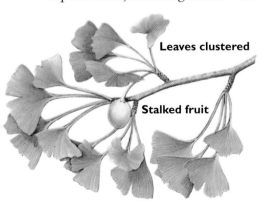

Leaves clustered

Stalked fruit

▲ The Maidenhair tree has fan-shaped leaves (look at fossil remains, right). The seed has a hard nutlike center.

◀ The Maidenhair tree, *Ginkgo biloba,* from China (left) and a fossil remain (below). This fossil is known as a living fossil because it is the only survivor of an ancient family of trees.

▼ Today, many familiar articles are made of plastic—from bags to artificial flowers. Yet the first plastic to be made completely from chemicals was not invented until 1907.

▶ Bakelite, an early kind of hard plastic, was invented in 1908 by Leo Baekeland. It was used for many household objects, such as those pictured here.

QUIZ

1. What was the first type of plastic to be invented?
2. What are today's two main kinds of plastic?
3. What plastic is used to make paints? And boats?
4. Name two of the ways plastic can be shaped.
5. What common household objects are made of vinyl?

(Answers on page 2176)

☼ PLASTIC

Plastic materials have become so numerous that you cannot go through a single day without touching something made of plastic. Toothbrushes, ballpoint pens, unbreakable dishes, cabinets and knobs for machines and appliances, light switches—all of these things and many more are made of plastic.

It seems hard to believe that before 1869, there was no such thing as plastic. The first plastic, *celluloid*, was invented in 1869 by John Wesley Hyatt. A $10,000 prize had been offered to anyone who invented a material that could replace ivory for making billiard balls. In his experiments, Hyatt dissolved nitrocellulose and camphor in alcohol. This produced a solid, white material that could be pressed into blocks. The celluloid blocks could then be cut and ground into billiard balls. Mr. Hyatt

won the prize and patented his invention. For more than 40 years afterward, Hyatt's celluloid was the only kind of plastic.

Manufacturers began making it into combs and brushes, buttons, piano keys, handles, and stiff collars and cuffs for men's shirts. Celluloid also became the main material for making plates for false teeth. The celluloid plastic was lighter and had less taste than the hard rubber that had previously been used to hold false teeth. George Eastman, a manufacturer of photographic equipment, invented a way to make celluloid film. Photographers until then had been taking pictures on chemically treated glass plates. Celluloid film aided Thomas Edison in his invention of the movie camera, which needed a continuous roll of film.

The main problem with celluloid was that it caught fire easily. In 1909, Leo Hendrik Baekeland, a Belgian chemist living in New Jersey, invented a new kind of plastic called *Bakelite*. Bakelite is hard to burn and impossible to melt. Telephone sets were among the first products made from Bakelite.

Since the early 1900s, many different plastics have been developed, each having a special characteristic or advantage that makes it good for various purposes. Some plastics stand heat better, while some withstand shock better. Some can be used in liquid form, and others can be spun into thread for making fabrics. Plastics are flexible. They can be

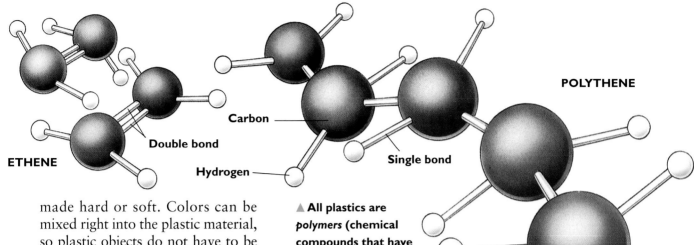

ETHENE

Double bond

Carbon

Hydrogen

Single bond

POLYTHENE

▲ **All plastics are *polymers* (chemical compounds that have very large molecules made up of thousands of smaller molecules). The smaller molecules join end to end and form long chains. This is the molecule for the plastic polythene, made from ethene gas molecules, which contain two carbon atoms and four hydrogen atoms.**

made hard or soft. Colors can be mixed right into the plastic material, so plastic objects do not have to be painted. Plastics are easily shaped and molded, and they can be used together with other materials, such as metal, wood, and rubber.

The two main types of plastic are *thermoplastic* and *thermosetting*. The thermoplastic types become soft and lose their shape in intense heat, and harden again when cooled. This group includes celluloids, nylon, and vinyls. The thermosetting types do not lose shape in heat but will keep their shape until destroyed. This group includes phenolics, ureas, and polyesters. The chemical process that makes plastic is called *polymerization*. The molecules of the plastic-making materials (oxygen, hydrogen, chlorine, nitrogen, and sulfur) form long chains called *polymers*. Different polymers determine the various kinds of plastics.

Plastics are shaped in a number of different ways. *Molding* is done by putting the plastic materials in molds under heat and pressure. The material is forced into all parts of the mold. The plastic takes the shape of the mold and then hardens. When the mold is opened, the plastic object is ready for use.

Casting is similar to molding, except that when the melted plastic is poured into the molds, no heat and pressure are needed. The plastic is allowed to cool, and then the mold is removed.

Extruding means "squeezing out." You extrude toothpaste from a tube, and the paste has the shape of the

tube's opening. Plastics softened by heat are extruded through a metal plate containing a hole of a particular shape. Plastic bars, tubes, and sheets are extruded. Extruded plastic can be *fabricated*—in other words shaped or carved by sawing, shaving, or drilling.

▼ **In the hot extrusion of plastics, the solid plastic pellet melts then is formed into shapes, when a large screw pushes it first through a heating chamber and then through a shaped opening.**

Plastic pellet

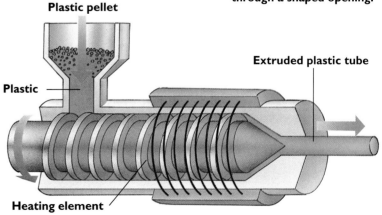

Extruded plastic tube

Plastic

Heating element

SOME PLASTICS

Name and Type of Plastic	Qualities	Some Products Manufactured from It
ACRYLIC (Thermoplastic)	Very strong. Withstands weathering and cold. Holds color well and is an excellent insulator. Has no odor or taste and is nonpoisonous.	Windows, eyeglass lenses and frames, signs, paints, storefronts, floor waxes, auto parts.
CELLULOSICS (Thermoplastic)	Four types: *Acetate, Butyrate, Ethyl Cellulose, Nitrate.* Strong, not easily scratched. Colorful, tasteless, nonpoisonous. Butyrate has slight odor but can be used outdoors. Nitrate is flammable.	*Acetate*—lampshades, toys, twine, vacuum-cleaner parts. *Butyrate*—underground pipe, tool handles. *Ethyl Cellulose*—camera cases, refrigerator and appliance parts. *Nitrate*—frames, table tennis balls, explosives.
EPOXY (Thermosetting)	Strong, hardens quickly. Not affected by heat, moisture, and chemicals. Resists weather well. Good adhesive qualities.	Paints, casting compounds, protective coatings, glues, adhesives, tools.
NYLON (Thermoplastic)	Strong, will not break if dropped. Can be sterilized by boiling. Good electrical insulator. Odorless, tasteless, nonpoisonous.	Fabrics, gears for machines, twine, spikes for athletic shoes, hinges, rollers, dishes, wire, insulation.
PHENOLIC (Thermosetting)	Withstands rough use and is hard to scratch. Good heat resistance and electrical insulation. Resists moisture well.	Handles for kitchenware, household appliances, electric tools, telephones, light plugs, switches.
POLYESTERS (Thermosetting)	Can be made into very large products, as strong as product requires. Not easily scratched or scarred. Not affected by weather or water. Withstands shock and impact well.	Boats, car bodies, furniture, roofing, bathtubs, air-conditioner cabinets, fishing tackle, roof tiles, fabrics.
POLYETHYLENE (Thermoplastic)	Can be used as liquid and in nonrigid forms. Seals out water but allows flow of oxygen. Can be sealed with heat. Comes in all colors as well as clear.	Plastic bags and food wrapping, squeeze bottles, athletic equipment, mixing bowls, bristles for brushes, ice trays, chair covers.
POLYSTYRENE (Thermoplastic)	Comes in all colors as well as clear. Resists very low temperatures. Seals out water. Good insulator. Surface wears well.	Wall tiles, toys, costume jewelry, shelves, freezer storage containers, dresser sets, refrigerator doors.
SILICONE (Thermosetting)	High elasticity. Can resist extreme heat and cold. Resists weather well. Used in electrical insulation.	Elastomer in electrical insulation, seals for jet engines and aircraft windows, waterproof cloth and paper, oven gaskets, greases.
UREA (Thermosetting)	Good insulator. Not affected by chemicals. Not easily broken or scratched.	Buttons, buckles, tops for tubes and jars, clock cases, light reflectors, picnic equipment.
VINYL (Thermoplastic)	Can be made rigid or flexible—sheets, tubes, liquids, etc. Resists tearing and water. Sealed with heat. Usually no odor or taste. Nonpoisonous.	Raincoats, phonograph records, garden hoses, table mats, door mats, curtains, boots, auto upholstery.

Calendering is putting a thin coat of heat-softened plastic on cloth. The coated cloth is put under pressure by running it through heated metal rollers. This presses the plastic into the fibers of the cloth. Products such as tablecloths, tents, and rainwear are made by calendering.

In *laminating,* a kind of sandwich is made by placing layers of plastic powder between layers of another material, such as wood or glass. The sandwich is put under heat and pressure. The plastic powder seals the layers of wood together, forming a strong sheet. Plywood and safety glass are made by lamination.

Although plastic is tough and flexible, it must still be treated with care.

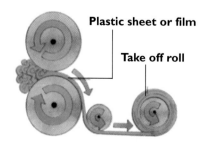

▶ *Calendering* is the method used to coat a flexible material, such as cloth, with a layer of plastic. The plastic is pressed onto the material by a system of rollers.

Plastic sheet or film

Take off roll

Certain hard plastics may break if dropped on a hard surface. Plastics cannot withstand rubbing with steel wool, sandpaper, or gritty cleansers. Their surfaces will become dull, scratched, and rough. Clean plastics with soap and damp cloths. Do not keep plastics, especially plastic toys, near heat or flames. Some plastics will burn rapidly, while others will melt.

If broken, most plastics can be readily repaired using adhesive.

▶▶▶▶ **FIND OUT MORE** ◀◀◀◀
Chemistry; Dies and Molds; Manufacturing; Synthetic

PLASTIC SURGERY

Until recently, people with bad injuries or burns had to accept that they would never recover fully. They might lose the use of parts of their body or have their appearance changed permanently. Modern plastic surgery means that there is new hope for such people.

Plastic surgery is a method of reshaping damaged or deformed parts of the body. This field of medicine lets people regain the use of parts of their body, or even improve their appearance.

One of the most important types of plastic surgery is *grafting*, which repairs damaged tissue by transferring healthy tissue to the injured area. Grafting is the method used to treat people with severe burns. A patch of healthy skin is taken from an unaffected part of the body, for example the buttocks or lower back. It is then used to replace the area that has been burned.

Other people can supply skin for a temporary graft if the injured person does not have enough for a skin graft. Skin from pigs or other animals can also be used for temporary grafts. These temporary grafts are replaced with full skin grafts when enough skin has grown back on the patient.

More complicated grafting transfers more than one type of tissue. These include nerves, bones, and blood vessels. Plastic surgeons can sometimes replace a severed arm or toe if they can renew all the tissue connections soon after the accident.

Plastic surgeons can also change the shape of parts of the body by rebuilding tissue in areas where it has been lost. An extreme example would be separating Siamese twins, but this method is used more often to correct birth defects such as a cleft lip.

Facelifts and nose jobs are examples of cosmetic plastic surgery that is used when people choose to change their own appearance. The methods of replacing or reshaping body tissue are the same that are used when plastic surgeons treat injuries.

▶▶▶▶ **FIND OUT MORE** ◀◀◀◀
Medicine; Skin; Surgery

▲ **A plastic surgeon separates layers of skin cells before sowing them on small samples of skin to grow large pieces for use in skin grafts. These skin grafts are used as permanent grafts for victims of extensive burns.**

PLATE TECTONICS

Plate tectonics is the theory that the Earth's crust consists of several giant, movable plates of solid rock that float on the Earth's mantle—liquid, *molten* (melted) rock—beneath the surface of the Earth. The movement of these plates is believed to cause the *continental drift* (slow movement of the land masses—continents—over the Earth's surface), earthquakes, and the formation of volcanoes and mountains.

200 million years ago

135 million years ago

Today

▲ The map of the world has changed greatly over the last 200 million years, as the continental plates have drifted apart.

Convection currents from the Earth's interior force molten rock to rise to the surface, spread over the ocean floor, and cool. At the same time, the molten rock spreads apart the heavy land masses. The plates push and slide against each other, bending, wrinkling, and causing geological changes. The theory of plate tectonics was first put forward by geologists in the 1960s.

▶ ▶ ▶ ▶ **FIND OUT MORE** ◀ ◀ ◀ ◀
Earth; Geology

PLATO (about 427–347 B.C.)

Most great thinkers in the Western world have been influenced by the ideas of the Greek philosopher, Plato. Plato thought deeply about all the major subjects that concern mankind. The questions he asked and the answers he suggested are still very meaningful to us today.

Plato was born in Athens, Greece. His real name was Aristocles. He was an excellent athlete as a youth and was given the nickname Plato, which means "broad-shouldered." He became a student of the Greek philosopher, Socrates, and was deeply influenced by his ideas. The execution of Socrates in 399 B.C. by the Athenian government was a bitter blow to Plato. He left Athens and spent several years traveling.

Plato returned to Athens in 387 B.C. and set up a school called the Academy. People traveled from distant countries to hear Plato's lectures on philosophy. One of his greatest pupils was the Greek philosopher, Aristotle.

Plato wrote down his ideas in the form of *dialogues*, or discussions between people. In most of these dialogues, Socrates is portrayed as the teacher. The dialogues explain Plato's ideas on subjects such as politics, law, science, education, art, and the nature of knowledge. One of the best known dialogues is *The Republic*, in which Plato describes his idea of an *ideal*, or perfect, government. He compares this government to an ideal person, who must be carefully educated to achieve qualities such as justice and wisdom.

▶ ▶ ▶ ▶ **FIND OUT MORE** ◀ ◀ ◀ ◀
Aristotle; Greece, Ancient; Philosophy; Socrates

PLATYPUS

The duck-billed platypus is a *monotreme*, an egg-laying mammal. Like most monotremes, it lives in Australia and Tasmania. The platypus has a leathery bill that looks like a duck's bill, and a tail that looks like a beaver's tail with fur on it. When fully grown, a platypus is 16 to 24 inches (40 to 60 cm) long and weighs up to 4 pounds (1.8 kg). The body is covered with a mixture of short, thick fur and long, shiny hairs. The legs are short and stubby and each webbed foot has five clawed toes. The male platypus has a poison spur on the ankle of each hind leg. The young platypus has small teeth, but adults have hornlike plates in their mouths for crushing and grinding food.

The platypus eats small fish and other animals it digs up from muddy stream bottoms, using its bill like a small shovel. It usually dives for food in the early morning and early evening. Normally it stays underwater for about a minute.

Platypuses live in burrows in the banks of streams and lakes. There

▶ A *bust* (sculptured head) of Plato, the Greek philosopher.

2106

◄ The eyes, ears, and nostrils of the platypus shut completely when the animal dives under water. Although the animal is blind and deaf in the water, its soft rubbery bill is so sensitive, the platypus has no difficulty in finding small creatures to eat.

are two kinds of burrows. One is the nest where the female platypus lays her eggs and takes care of her babies. The other burrow is where the male lives, and where the female lives when she is not having babies.

The female platypus lays from one to three soft, leathery eggs, each less than an inch (2.5 cm) long. When the baby platypus hatches, it is blind and without fur. The mother platypus "sweats" milk into the fur of her belly, and the babies lick it. The young platypuses live in the burrow for four months, until they are almost fully grown.

The platypus has few natural enemies, and it may live to be 15 or more years old. However, in recent times, people killed many platypuses for their skins, and the species almost died out. Now there are strict laws against hunting them, and the platypus is no longer in any danger of becoming extinct.

▶▶▶▶ **FIND OUT MORE** ◄◄◄◄
Animal; Australia;
Australian
Mammals; Mammal

PLUMBING

The system of tubs, basins, pipes, and drains that brings water into our homes and carries it away is called *plumbing*. A plumbing system consists of two parts—the *piping* and the *fixtures*. Piping is usually hidden beneath floors and walls. It carries the water to and from the fixtures. Fixtures are the parts of a plumbing system you can see. They include sinks, bathtubs, drinking fountains, and toilets. They may be made of porcelain, glass, copper, steel, or plastic. The word *plumbing* comes from the Latin word *plumbum*, which means "lead."

The first known plumbing system was in Egypt. It used lead piping. Romans later used clay tiles and stone, as well as lead. Thomas Jefferson designed one of the first indoor plumbing systems in the United States in the late 1700s. But most Americans had no indoor plumbing until later.

Today, most people have indoor plumbing. Most houses and buildings are connected to a public water supply, but some homes, especially those in rural areas, get water from a

The Minoans main engineering achievement was their clever water supply. More than 3,500 years ago, the people living in the palace at Knossos had piped fresh water to bathrooms and bathtubs, and even used a kind of flushing toilet.

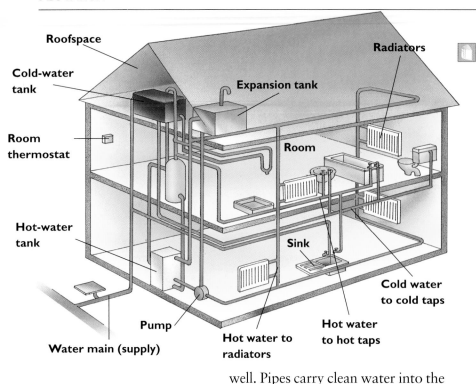

Roofspace

Cold-water tank

Room thermostat

Hot-water tank

Pump

Water main (supply)

Expansion tank

Radiators

Room

Sink

Cold water to cold taps

Hot water to hot taps

Hot water to radiators

▲ A diagram showing a plumbing system in a house. Hot and cold water is piped around the house to the taps and radiators.

▲ This painting of Plutarch, the Greek writer, was made sometime during the 1400s.

well. Pipes carry clean water into the house and to the kitchen, the bathroom, and the laundry. Some of the water goes into a tank to be heated. Supplying clean water is the easier part of plumbing. Getting rid of dirty water and wastes is more difficult. Plumbing must be designed to keep waste out of the clean water supplies. Sewer gas and sewage are poisonous. Faulty plumbing that lets wastes enter the water people drink can start and spread diseases.

Water traps (the U-shaped pipes under each sink) keep sewer gas from entering homes. Water collects in the curve of the pipe and blocks the sewer gas from escaping through the sink drain. Vent pipes carry the gas to the roof, where it escapes into the air. Waste water is carried through a drain pipe into a sewer to be carried away from the house. In rural areas, water drains into a septic tank buried outside the house. Kitchen waste contains grease, which can combine with soapy water to block the sewers. Some kitchen sinks have grease traps that collect the grease and let the water run through. They must be cleaned occasionally.

▶▶▶▶ **FIND OUT MORE** ◀◀◀◀
Water Pollution; Water Supply

PLUTARCH
(about A.D. 46–120)

Plutarch was a Greek writer and teacher. His greatest works are a series of *biographies* (stories of people's lives) and essays. Plutarch was born in the city of Chaeronea, Greece. He was educated in Athens and became a teacher and a writer. Plutarch studied philosophy in Athens, and he later lectured on this subject in Rome. After returning to Chaeronea, he also worked as a government official and was later made a priest of Apollo. Plutarch's *Moralia* is a collection of about 78 thoughtful essays on many different subjects.

His best-known work is *Parallel Lives*, which contains 50 biographies of outstanding Greek and Roman soldiers, legislators, orators, and statesmen. Most of the biographies are written in pairs—one Greek and one Roman. The lives and accomplishments of the two persons are compared. *Parallel Lives* was translated into English in the 1500s. The English dramatist William Shakespeare based several of his plays on stories from Plutarch's biographies. *Parallel Lives* tells us a great deal about the history of ancient Greece and Rome in an entertaining way.

▶▶▶▶ **FIND OUT MORE** ◀◀◀◀
Greek Literature

PLUTO

SEE SOLAR SYSTEM

PLUTONIUM

SEE NUCLEAR ENERGY, RADIOACTIVITY

PLYMOUTH COLONY

SEE PILGRIM SETTLERS

POCAHONTAS
(about 1595–1617)

Pocahontas was a Native American princess, the daughter of Powhatan. Powhatan was the chief of the Chickahominy tribe that lived along the coast of Virginia when the English settlers first arrived there. "Pocahontas" was a nickname, meaning "playful one"—Pocahontas's real name was Matoaka.

Powhatan ruled a confederacy of Algonkian-speaking Native Americans. They fought to stop the settlers from taking their land. According to legend, Pocahontas saved the life of Captain John Smith, who was the leader of the English colony at

Jamestown. When he was captured by the Native Americans, Pocahontas stopped her father's warriors from clubbing him to death. Later, in 1613, Pocahontas was kidnapped by the settlers and held as a hostage to prevent Powhatan from attacking the colony. She was converted to Christianity and baptized with the name Rebecca. In 1614, she married John Rolfe, a colonial leader. This brought peace between the colonists and the Native Americans until 1618, when Powhatan died.

Pocahontas went with her husband to England in 1616. She had a son, Thomas. She died of smallpox on her way back to Virginia in 1617.

▶▶▶▶ **FIND OUT MORE** ◀◀◀◀
American Colonies; Jamestown;
Native Americans; Powhatan

POE, EDGAR ALLAN
(1809–1849)

Edgar Allan Poe was one of America's greatest writers. He wrote poems, essays, short stories, and criticism. Poe was born in Boston. His parents were both actors. His father left the family when Poe was only a year old, and his mother died when he was 3 years old. John Allan, a Virginia merchant, and his wife raised Poe as a foster child. While he was at college, Poe received little money to live on and turned to gambling. He quarreled with his foster father and was forced to leave college because of his debts. Poe started writing and published his first work, *Tamerlane and Other Poems,* in 1827.

Poe wrote some of the first detective stories. He also wrote mystery and horror stories. "The Fall of the House of Usher," "The Tell-Tale Heart," "The Gold Bug," and "The Pit and the Pendulum" are among his most famous short stories. Poe's work and his ideas about writing and mankind influenced many other writers, including T. S. Eliot, James Joyce, and André Gide.

Poe married his cousin. They had no children. After his wife's death, Poe became extremely sad and sometimes drank heavily to relieve his grief. Found unconscious on a street in Baltimore, Maryland, Poe later died in a hospital.

▶▶▶▶ **FIND OUT MORE** ◀◀◀◀
Literature

POETRY

Poetry is the oldest form of literature. It probably began when primitive people started to chant or sing in time to the beating of a drum. Before people developed a system of writing, they found that the best way to remember a story was to sing it or put it in a

▼ A portrait of Edgar Allan Poe, a talented and imaginative American writer.

◀ In 1613, Pocahontas was captured by the English settlers, taken to Jamestown, and baptized Rebecca.

Edgar Allan Poe created the first ever private detective hero in his novels *The Purloined Letter, The Murders in the Rue Morgue,* and *The Mystery of Marie Roget.*

▲ John Keats, one of the greatest British poets of the Romantic period, in the early part of the 1800s.

When the famous writer Samuel Johnson was asked what poetry is, he replied: "Why, Sir, it is much easier to say what it is not. We all *know* what light is, but it is not easy to *tell* what it is."

▼ Sylvia Plath (below) and Ezra Pound (below right), two great American poets of the 20th century. Both authors wrote poems about personal experiences in their own lives.

certain rhythmical pattern. In this way, poetry was born. Poems were sung or recited for thousands of years before they were ever written down, and reading a poem aloud is still often the best way to appreciate it fully.

Poetry is a form of literature that uses words in more rhythmical patterns than any other kind of writing or speech. Poetry is like music in that it creates beautiful sounds—but poetry creates them with words. Poetry expresses emotions and ideas in vivid language that excites your imagination and makes you see the poem's subject more clearly or see it in a different way.

Much poetry is written in *rhyme*. Rhyme means that the words at the end of the poem's lines sound alike. Here is an example of a simple rhyme 1:1

The world is so full of a number of *things*,
I'm sure we should all be as happy as *kings*.

"Things" and "kings" rhyme. Rhyme is not necessary in poetry, however. The use of rhyme simply depends on what the poet prefers. Many poets use rhyme in some poems but not in others.

Rhythm in poetry is the pattern of sound variations—loud, soft, long, short—that the poet uses to create a sense of movement. In speaking, louder and longer sounds are naturally stressed more than other sounds. When you read a poem aloud, you can feel the kind of movement the poet intended. If the poem is happy, you may feel as if you're

▲ The Greek poet Sappho wrote about love and jealousy between the women she lived with on the island of Lesbos.

running or skipping as you read. If the poem is sad, it may seem to move very slowly. Read these lines aloud, and feel the movement:

'Twas the night before Christmas, and all through the house,
Not a creature was stirring, not even a mouse.

This is called *metrical verse*, meaning "measured." Meter has a regular, precise, rhythmical pattern. It is based on the *foot*, a group of one stressed sound and one or two unstressed sounds. (The sounds in each kind of foot are arranged in a certain order.) Every line of metrical verse contains a specific number of feet. When a poem is written in meter, words are arranged so that the stressed and unstressed sounds will fall into the chosen rhythmical pattern. In the example above, each line consists of four feet. Each foot is made up of two unstressed sounds and one stressed sound. ("'Twas the night" is one foot.) This example is rhymed, but metrical verse does not have to rhyme. If a poem has no regular pattern or rhythm, it is called *free verse*. Free verse also does not have to rhyme.

The three major types of poetry are narrative, lyric, and dramatic. *Narrative poetry* tells a story. It includes epic poems, which are long tales, usually drawn from history, legend, or myth, about some heroic deed. The *ballad* is another sort of narrative poem. It is shorter and is often sung. *Lyric poetry* tells of the poet's own feelings and thoughts. Lyric poems were once sung to the musical accompaniment of a stringed instrument called the "lyre," after which the poetry was named. Lyric poems include sonnets, odes, and elegies. A *sonnet* is a poem of 14 lines with a specific rhyming pattern. (For example, one line must always rhyme with a certain other line, and so on.) An *ode* is written in praise of something, such as a glowing sunset or a beautiful old vase. An *elegy* is a sad poem written in memory of someone who has died. *Dramatic poetry* has characters who tell a story through dialogue, just as a play does.

Poetry has been enjoyed all over the world for thousands of years. More than 700 years ago, the Japanese began writing a form of poetry called *haiku*. A Japanese haiku has only three lines and usually consists of 17 syllables. The first line has 5 syllables, the second line 7, and the third line 5. Haiku have become very popular with American poets. Read the examples below of haiku written by Japanese poets, then try writing haiku of your own.

A baby warbler
gaily swinging upside down
sings his first song.
                    KIKAKU

The tight string broke and
the loose kite fell fluttering,
losing its spirit.
                    KUBONTA

A cloud shimmering
on the still pool...a fish stirs
under the water.
                    SHURIN

Poems can tell long stories or describe a single second. The love of poetry begins when a baby is charmed by a nursery rhyme. But no one ever grows too old to love the beauty that comes from a poem.

▶▶▶▶ **FIND OUT MORE** ◀◀◀◀
Literature

LEARN BY DOING

Haiku holds within it a whole mood or thought. It tells of one moment captured from life. When it is read, that moment comes alive again. Haiku can be fun—try writing one! Look around for something that pleases you. It might be the soft fur of a kitten. It could be a raindrop rolling very, very slowly, then suddenly fast, down a wet windowpane. Or an oily patch of water on a city street reflecting all the colors of a rainbow. Look closely at the world around you, then carefully choose your words.

POISON

A *poison* is any substance that damages or destroys living tissue. It is a substance that will kill you or make you very sick if you swallow it, breathe it, or take it into your body through your skin. It is difficult to define a poison very accurately because almost any substance is poisonous if we take in enough. Some things are poisonous even in very small amounts. Alkaloids, which are in poisonous mushrooms, can kill a person if he or she eats only a very small amount. Other things are poisonous only in large amounts, and are harmless or even good for you in small amounts. Small amounts of a drug that slows the heartbeat are good for a person with certain kinds of heart disease. A large amount of the same drug is poisonous, because it will stop the heart altogether.

Some things found in almost every household are poisonous if they are swallowed. Among these are lye, ammonia, bleach, and iodine.

To help a person who has taken a poison, you should quickly:

1. CALL A DOCTOR, 911, OR A POISON CONTROL CENTER.
2. GIVE AN ANTIDOTE.
3. KEEP THE POISONED PERSON WARM.

Don't try to take the poisoned person to the doctor instead of calling. You may not have time. If you cannot talk to a doctor immediately, call

The most deadly poison produced by any animal comes from the skin of the Koboi arrow-poison frog that lives in Colombia, South America. An ounce of the poison could kill more than two million people.

▶ **The symbol for poisonous substances is a skull and crossbones.**

POISONOUS SUBSTANCES

Some **household substances** may be poisonous if swallowed. Furniture polish, gasoline, lighter fluid, and kerosene are among these. So are lye, drain cleaner, bleach, dishwasher detergent, and toilet cleaner.

Corrosive poisons include acids and alkalies.

Irritant poisons include hydrogen sulfide and household ammonia.

Systemic poisons include antifreeze.

Poison gases include carbon monoxide, a gas given off by car exhausts and poorly ventilated coal stoves.

Taken in excess, many **drugs and medicines** can be poisonous, including aspirin and sleeping pills.

Garden and farm **insecticides** and **weed killers** can kill.

Snake venom is only poisonous if it gets into the bloodstream through a bite (not if swallowed).

Poisonous plants include holly (berries), locoweed (leaves, flowers, nectar, and seeds), lily of the valley (all parts), hydrangea (leaves and buds), and deadly nightshade (all parts).

---

a *poison control center.* Many states have such places that you can phone to find out what to do about poisoning. The public health, police, or fire departments of your town can give you a list of poison control centers and their phone numbers. You should have this list in your home. If you do not know what number to call, dial 911 or 0 for the telephone operator, who will connect you with the proper authority.

An *antidote* is a substance that combines chemically with the poison and stops its action. If a person has swallowed lye, antidotes are half a glass of vinegar mixed with half a glass of water, or several glasses of lemon, orange, or grapefruit juice. For a "universal" antidote, good for most poisons, mix milk of magnesia, strong tea, and crumbled burned toast.

Sometimes it is best to get the poison out of a person's stomach before giving an antidote. To do this, you must make the person vomit. The easiest way is to tickle the inside of his or her upper throat with your finger. Or dissolve a tablespoon of salt in a glassful of lukewarm water and make the poisoned person drink four glassfuls, one right after the other. A drink that causes vomiting, such as this one, is called an *emetic*.

It is NOT always good to make a poisoned person vomit. If the person has swallowed a poison such as lye, which burned the mouth and throat, he or she should not be made to vomit. As it comes up, it will burn the mouth and throat a second time. In order to know whether to

make a person vomit, read a chart that tells you what to do in case someone is poisoned. You should have such a chart on the wall of some room in your home. You can get a chart from the United States Public Health Service in Washington, D.C. You probably can obtain one from your town's public health service also. Ask your teacher how to get one.

▶▶▶▶ **FIND OUT MORE** ◀◀◀◀
Mushroom; Poisonous Plant

POISONOUS PLANT

A poisonous plant may be poisonous to touch, or it may be poisonous to eat. Whether a plant is poisonous to touch or eat depends on the kind of poison it contains and where the poison is. (If the poison is right inside the plant, it will not be poisonous to touch.) How poisonous it is depends on how strong the poison is and how much poison the plant contains.

Very few plants are completely poisonous. Some plants are poisonous only in certain seasons or at certain stages of their development. The *cocklebur* is poisonous only at the seedling stage. Often only a part of a plant is poisonous. Some common foods come from plants that are partly poisonous. The leaf blades of rhubarb are poisonous and so are potato leaves.

The best known poisonous plant is *poison ivy*. It contains an oil called *urushiol* that can irritate the skin, causing itching and blistering. Poison ivy can be recognized by its three shiny, jagged leaflets on each leaf stalk and by its white berries. To help you recognize poison ivy, remember this saying: "One, two, three, watch out for me!" *Poison oak* and *poison sumac* are closely related to poison ivy, and contain similar poisons. Poison oak also has three leaflets and white berries, but its leaves are shaped like oak leaves. However, poison oak is not really an oak. Poison ivy and poison oak are both vines. Poison sumac is a shrub that can grow as high as 20 feet (6 m). It has 7 to 13 leaflets and white berries.

If you should ever touch poison ivy, poison oak, or poison sumac, wash the oil off quickly with strong laundry soap or detergent. Do not use ordinary bathroom soaps. These will only spread the oil and the itching. Cover the itching skin with a lotion and try not to scratch.

The best protection against poison ivy and other plants that can irritate the skin is not to touch them. If you go walking in the woods, make sure your arms and legs are covered and don't touch strange plants. Don't try to burn poison ivy—even the smoke is poisonous.

Plants that are poisonous to eat are more common than plants that are poisonous to touch. Many mushrooms and green plants contain poisons that attack the nerves, muscles, blood, or organs of the body. The *fly amanita* is a pretty mushroom with a white-spotted red cap, but it contains a poison that at-

tacks the brain. Another amanita mushroom is called *destroying angel*. Its poison attacks the liver and the kidneys, and there is no known cure for it.

Many plants that are grown because of their beauty are poisonous. The *oleander* is often planted in gardens and along roadsides. Its leaves are poisonous if swallowed or chewed. Many animals and a few children die every year from oleander poisoning. *Bloodroot, lily of the valley,* and *larkspur* are other common poisonous plants. *Deadly nightshade* is yet another highly poisonous plant, but also has medicinal uses as a sedative. The deadliest plant poison is contained in the seeds of the *rosary pea*.

Many plants that are not considered poisonous can still make you very sick. There is no rule that will tell you how to recognize all the poisonous plants that grow in woods, fields, and gardens. The best rule to follow is never to eat, and try not to touch, any part of a plant unless you are absolutely sure it is safe to do so.

▶▶▶▶ **FIND OUT MORE** ◀◀◀◀
Plant; Poison

Poison ivy

▲ **Poison ivy can cause skin irritation if it is touched. This is because its leaves contain a poisonous oil.**

Deadly nightshade

▲ **The deadly nightshade plant is extremely poisonous. It contains alkaloids that attack the nervous system and can even cause death.**

▼ **A selection of poisonous toadstools and mushrooms. These should never be eaten.**

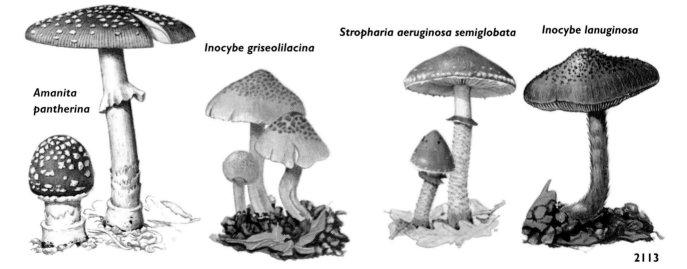

Amanita pantherina

Inocybe griseolilacina

Stropharia aeruginosa semiglobata

Inocybe lanuginosa

POLAND

Capital city
Warsaw
(1,649,000 people)

Area
120,725 square miles
(312,677 sq. km)

Population
38,064,000 people

Government
Multiparty republic

Natural resources
Coal, sulfur, copper, natural gas, silver, lead

Export products
Machinery and equipment, fuels, minerals, metals, manufactured consumer goods, chemicals

Unit of money
Zloty

Official language
Polish

Thousands of Polish non-Jews were killed by Nazis. Many more were sent to forced labor camps.

POLAND

The Baltic Sea and part of Russia make up the northern border of Poland, a country in north central Europe. Belarus is to the east and Germany is to the west. The Czech and Slovak republics border Poland on the south. Much of Poland lies in valleys made by rivers that flow to the sea. The main river is the Vistula. The country has many lakes and forests. The only tall mountains in Poland are the rugged Carpathians in the south. These contain many minerals, including salt and coal.

Most people in Poland are descended from the Polians, a Slavic tribe. The Slavs were wandering tribes that lived in the forests of Eastern Europe in prehistoric times. Poland once extended from the Baltic Sea to the Black Sea. Wars with Russia and other neighbors resulted in continual changes in Poland's boundaries. Several times it was *partitioned* (divided) between its more powerful neighbors after wars. In fact, Poland once disappeared from the map of Europe altogether. After World War I, it became an independent country again. During World War II, Poland suffered from invasion and occupation by Germany and the former Soviet Union. Many thousands of Polish Jews died in Nazi concentration camps. In 1945, after the war, the Russians set up a Communist government. Poland became the Polish People's Republic.

Before the destruction of much of Poland in World War II, most of the people were farmers. Now only about one-fifth of the people *till* (plow) the land. The main agricultural products are rye, potatoes, wheat, barley, oats, sugar beets, and hogs. Although there are cooperatives, state farms, and agricultural associations, many farmers own small plots. Factories owned by the state produce machinery, fertilizers, textiles, chemicals, iron and steel products, and electronic equipment.

BALTIC SEA

© 1994 GeoSystems, an R.R. Donnelley & Sons Company

Warsaw is the capital of Poland and an important industrial center.

Although religion was not encouraged by the Communist government, 90 percent of Poles are Roman Catholics. The people have sought greater freedoms in recent years, particularly the right to form free labor unions. The Solidarity labor union became a center of opposition to the government in the early 1980s, and in 1989, free elections swept Solidarity candidates into power. Poland had a noncommunist-led government for the first time in 50 years.

▶▶▶▶ **FIND OUT MORE** ◀◀◀◀
World War I; World War II

POLAR LIFE

Late in 1967, Peter J. Barrett of Ohio State University was exploring Graphite Peak, a mountain in Antarctica, the continent at the South Pole. He found a fossil bone. The fossil was examined by Edwin H. Colbert of the American Museum of Natural History. He said it belonged to a *labyrinthodont,* a prehistoric animal and one of the earliest animals that lived for short periods out of water. Labyrinthodonts were animals of hot climates, so millions of years ago, Antarctica must have been closer to the equator. Scientists found many more fossils that showed Antarctica was once warm and full of living things.

This may seem strange when you think of Antarctica's icy wastes today, but the continent still has a large animal population. The best-known land animals are penguins. Also found in the waters around Antarctica are many seals and whales. All these creatures must eat fish and other sea life, because there are almost no plants at all in Antarctica. No people live there (except scientists).

Surrounding the North Pole is the Arctic Ocean, which is frozen over. Also near the North Pole are some very cold areas of land: Greenland, northern North America, and the tundra of northern Russia. In these regions, there are polar bears on the ice, and seals and fish beneath it. There are also people, the Eskimos (Inuits). Tundra regions have some plant life—mosses, dwarf shrubs, some flowers, and a few stunted trees. Animals of the tundra include Arctic fox, elk (moose), and reindeer (caribou).

One bird that seems to like both

◀ The market square of Warsaw, Poland's capital. The square was rebuilt in its original style after it was destroyed during World War II.

▼ The polar lands: the Arctic (below left) and the Antarctic (below right). The Arctic consists mainly of a treeless land, called the *tundra*. It has many more animals than the Antarctic, because the snow melts in the summer and animals can feed on the plants growing there. The Antarctic is an icy land surrounded by cold seas. Even in summer most of the land is covered with ice. Most of the animals there live in the sea. They feed on fish and other sea creatures.

WHERE TO DISCOVER MORE

Beattie, Owen. *Buried in Ice*. New York: Scholastic, 1992.

Pringle, Laurence P. *Antarctica: The Last Unspoiled Continent*. New York: Simon & Schuster Books, 1992.

▶ **Boston motorcycle police survey a scene beside their powerful and fast motorcycles.**

▲ **The first London police force was set up in 1740. The members were known as *Bow Street Runners*, and were so effective in their job that criminals feared them.**

polar regions is the Arctic tern. It lives and breeds in and around the Arctic during the northern summer. It then migrates to the Antarctic regions during the southern summer.

▶▶▶▶ **FIND OUT MORE** ◀◀◀◀
Antarctica; Arctic; Bear; Continental Drift; Deer; Eskimo; Fossil; Fox; Migration; North Pole; Penguin; Seals and Sea Lions; Tundra; Whales and Whaling

POLICE

Police are uniformed men and women employed by a government to protect the lives and property of the people in a community. They try to enforce laws, prevent crimes, and keep things running smoothly. Some police officers, such as detectives, usually do not wear uniforms.

History
Since early times, people have felt the need for protection and regulation of society. This need has resulted in the development of police forces. In ancient societies, warriors acted as police and enforced rules of the tribe. The early Roman emperors appointed a special force to police the city of Rome. The French emperor Charlemagne organized a police force in A.D. 800.

The Anglo-Saxons (people who lived in England in early times) developed a system of protection based on groupings of families. Every hundred families elected a *reeve* as its leader and protector. The reeve of a *shire*, or county, became known as a *shire reeve*, which was shortened to *sheriff*. Each sheriff organized an informal police force to protect the shire. The sheriff system came to the United States with the English colonists. It was used in most American cities and towns until the 1800s, and is still used in some small towns today.

Boston set up a small force of paid

daytime police in 1838. In 1845, New York became the first American city to establish a large, day-and-night police force.

Police Organization
Today, there are police departments in every city, county, and state in the United States. Each department is responsible to a certain level of government—local, state, or national—instead of taking orders from just one national office.

A small country town might have a small police department with one or two officers. A large city like New York or Los Angeles might have many thousands of police officers. Large cities are usually divided into districts, referred to as *precincts*.

Each precinct has its own police station. The head of the police department in a large city is known as the police chief or the police commissioner. Officers who rank below are the chief inspector, deputy inspectors, captains, lieutenants, and sergeants. Nonranking police officers are called patrol officers.

Most big city police departments have separate divisions for different kinds of police work. For example, the traffic division directs traffic and gives tickets to traffic offenders. The criminal laboratory analyzes chemical evidence. Police chemists in the laboratory might test food to see if it contains poison. Detectives investigate crimes or look for clues to find a certain wanted suspect.

County police departments serve an entire county. They are usually run by a sheriff, who also operates the county jail. Every state has some type of state police or state highway patrol force. State police can operate throughout the state.

Federal police agencies try to find people who have violated federal laws. They work closely with local police departments to catch criminals. The Federal Bureau of Investigation (FBI), the Secret Service, the Internal Revenue Service, the Bureau of Customs, the Bureau of Narcotics, and the Coast Guard all have police agents.

Every country has its own type of police. Some European countries have centralized police forces. This means that local police are under the control of a national bureau.

Police Officers and Their Work

If a person wants to become a police officer in the United States, he or she must have a high school diploma and pass a civil service test. He or she must also be in good health and have no criminal record. Most federal agencies and some local police departments today require applicants to have done some college work. Once accepted into the force, police officers enter a stiff training program. They learn what the laws are and how to give first aid. They are taught the police regulations of their city and how to use weapons.

A police officer works in shifts. He or she might work the day shift from 8 A.M. to 4 P.M., or a night shift starting at midnight and ending at 8 A.M. A police officer begins the day with a roll call at the station house. Then he or she receives instructions from the captain. Throughout the day, police officers report back to the station

house from telephone call boxes or by means of a radio system. Through the radio system, they can be informed of crimes, accidents, or dangerous situations and go directly to the scene. Police officers in patrol cars have radios installed in their cars. While on patrol, they help people in many ways. They give directions to those who are lost. They may take someone home who is sick or has gotten hurt, or they may take

▼ A police officer stands beside his highway patrol vehicle. He is checking traffic speeds and driver behavior, and is looking out for stolen vehicles and anything else suspicious.

that person to the hospital. Police officers direct traffic to prevent accidents, and they sometimes help children cross the street on their way home from school. Police officers look for stolen cars and watch out for fights and burglaries.

All police officers must train their

◄ The police are trained to deal with crowds—whether it is keeping an eye on demonstrations, keeping order at ball games, or, as shown here, keeping the public away from a danger zone.

▲ A policewoman on duty in Washington. There are on average two law enforcement officers for about every 1,000 U.S. citizens.

▶ In the United States, Presidential candidates are selected at political conventions.

▲ A political cartoon makes fun of the Presidential campaign of 1912. Woodrow Wilson, who won, rides the Democratic donkey; William Howard Taft sits atop the Republican elephant; and Theodore Roosevelt is astride the Progressive Party's bull moose.

minds to be alert to unusual activities. They must be able to decide quickly how to handle any type of situation. A police officer's work is very difficult and often dangerous. He or she must be ready to help people at all times, even if it means risking his or her own life. Understanding and communication between the people in a community and the police force are very important. Police will be able to do their work best if they have the support of the people in their community.

▶▶▶▶ **FIND OUT MORE** ◀◀◀◀
Coast Guard; Crime; Customs; Detective; Federal Bureau of Investigation; Fingerprint; Fire Fighting; Government; Judo; Law; Safety

POLITICAL PARTY

Politics includes everything from campaigning for election (your own or someone else's) to working with elected officials to make sure your interests are represented in government—on the local (city or county), state, and national levels. People have found that their views on important issues have more influence with other voters, and with the government, if they organize into political parties. Large numbers of people working for a common goal have more power than one individual working for the same goal.

Political parties nominate a set of candidates for current elections (local, state, and national) who will work for their interests if elected. Political parties write down their viewpoints and aims in a party *platform*. They make sure their views and candidates are well-known and encourage voters to support them. Party members work at the polls during elections. When a party's candidate is elected, the party can recommend to him or her people for

certain jobs. (Those who have actively supported a candidate are more likely to receive job appointments when that candidate is elected.)

The United States Constitution does not require any political organizations. But political parties have existed since the beginning of the nation. People in the United States have found political parties to be the most effective and best organized method of seeking control of the government. There are two major parties in the United States: the Democratic and the Republican parties. Some smaller parties exist, but they are not very powerful. Sometimes a third party will support a candidate from one of the two major parties in return for the promised support of some of the third party's goals. People are also free to run for

office as independent candidates when no party backs them.

Canada also has a two-party system. Other countries, such as Britain, France, Italy, and Japan, have several powerful major parties. Some countries, such as China, and many countries in Africa and Latin America, have only one political party.

▶▶▶▶ **FIND OUT MORE** ◀◀◀◀
Capitalism; Communism; Democracy; Dictator; Election; Fascism; Parliament; Presidency; Republic; Socialism

POLK, JAMES KNOX
(1795–1849)

"Fifty-four forty or fight!" was the campaign slogan of James K. Polk, who became the eleventh President of the United States. Polk was determined to obtain the entire Oregon Territory from Great Britain, up to the latitude 54 degrees, 40 minutes. He was finally forced to compromise with the British, and the boundary between the United States and Canada was set at the 49th parallel.

Polk was born in Mecklenburg County in North Carolina. He was the oldest of the ten children of a wealthy farmer. He graduated with honors from the University of North Carolina and went to Nashville, Tennessee, to study law. There Polk met former President Andrew Jackson, who encouraged him to go into politics. At the age of 28, Polk was elected to the Tennessee state legislature and, two years later, to the U.S. House of Representatives. Polk served as a representative until 1839, acting as speaker of the House after 1835. He was elected governor of Tennessee in 1839. In 1844, partly due to Jackson's influence, the Democratic party nominated Polk for President.

Polk was a "dark horse" candidate. This means that he was not well-known, and his nomination had not been expected. Polk's name was not familiar to many Democrats outside of Tennessee. An amusing story is told about how one loyal party member received the news of Polk's nomination. "Hurrah," he shouted. "Hurrah for—what did you say his name was?"

Polk proved to be an efficient president, but he was not a popular one. In 1845, the United States annexed Texas, but Mexico refused to give up its claims to Texas and other territories in the Southwest. Negotiations between the United States and Mexico failed. Polk then sent U.S. troops to occupy territory in Texas and, in 1846, asked Congress to declare war on Mexico. The Mexican War (1846–1848) ended in an American victory. Mexico gave up Texas and later agreed to sell to the United States most of the territory west of Texas, including California. The territory of Oregon was also formed during Polk's administration.

Polk refused to be nominated for a second term. His health had suffered during his four years as President. He looked forward to retiring to Polk Place, a mansion he had bought in Nashville. He spent only a few months there before he died.

▶▶▶▶ **FIND OUT MORE** ◀◀◀◀
Jackson, Andrew; Mexican War; Oregon

**JAMES KNOX POLK
ELEVENTH PRESIDENT**

**MARCH 4, 1845–
MARCH 3, 1849**

Born: November 2, 1795, Mecklenburg County, North Carolina
Parents: Samuel and Jane Knox Polk
Education: University of North Carolina
Religion: Presbyterian
Occupation: Lawyer
Political party: Democratic
State represented: Tennessee
Married: 1824 to Sarah Childress (1803–1891)
Children: None
Died: June 15, 1849, Nashville, Tennessee
Buried: State Capitol, Nashville, Tennessee

◀ At the end of the Mexican War, the U.S. gained parts of Arizona, California, Colorado, Nevada, New Mexico, Utah, and Wyoming.

**WHERE TO
DISCOVER MORE**

Hoff, Mary King. *Rivers and Lakes*. Minneapolis, MN: Lerner Publications, 1991.
Pringle, Laurence P. *Global Warming*. New York: Arcade Publications, 1990.

POLLINATION

SEE FLOWER, PLANT, REPRODUCTION

POLLUTION

In 1986, water, which had been used to fight a huge fire at a chemical factory in Switzerland, poured into the Rhine River. The water was poisoned by the chemicals. The poison killed fish and made the water unfit to drink. The most important European river had become polluted.

This is an extreme example, but pollution is all around us. When you throw a candy wrapper on the ground, instead of putting it in a trash can, you are contributing to pollution. There are several forms of pollution. The main ones are:

AIR POLLUTION. Many factories pour poisonous fumes and chemicals, such as nitrogen dioxide and sulfur dioxide, into the air from their chimneys. Automobiles and airplanes release nitrogen dioxide and carbon monoxide from their exhausts. Particles in the air may keep the sun's heat from the ground or may prevent it from escaping back into space, thus heating up the Earth. This heating-up is called the greenhouse effect.

WATER POLLUTION. Sewage and waste water from factories pour into our rivers and lakes. Water from farmland carries chemicals such as weed killers and insecticides.

SOIL POLLUTION is produced by the dumping of farm and industrial wastes, fertilizers, weed killers, and insecticides. Solid waste matter—like a candy wrapper—that takes a long time to *decay* (rot), also causes pollution.

NOISE is also a form of pollution—from airplanes, traffic, and even radios!

Air pollution has been reduced in some areas. Burning low-sulfur oil and coal in power plants and factories has reduced the pollution in many cities. To meet federal standards, automobile engines have been redesigned and now cars are fitted with catalytic converters that greatly reduce the pollutants in exhausts. But much still has to be done, and vast amounts of money will have to be spent to keep the Earth clean.

▶▶▶▶ **FIND OUT MORE** ◀◀◀◀
Air Pollution; Chemistry; Fertilizer; Greenhouse Effect; Water Pollution

▼ Pollution is caused by factories, power plants, cars, and agriculture releasing waste chemicals into the air, earth, and water.

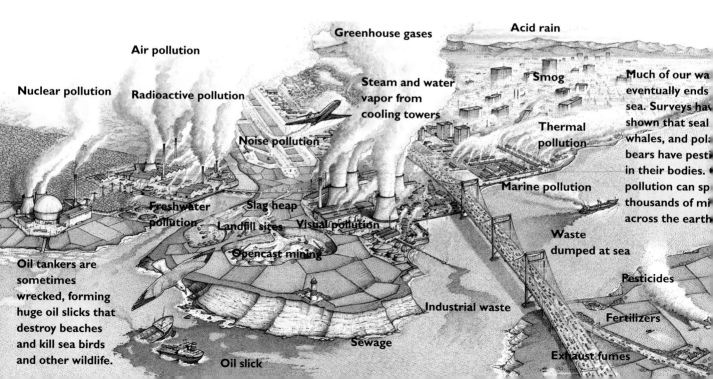

Oil tankers are sometimes wrecked, forming huge oil slicks that destroy beaches and kill sea birds and other wildlife.

Much of our wa[ste] eventually ends [up in the] sea. Surveys hav[e] shown that seal[s], whales, and pol[ar] bears have pesti[cides] in their bodies. [This] pollution can sp[read] thousands of mi[les] across the earth[.]

POLO

Polo is a game similar to field hockey, but played on horseback. There are four players on a polo team. Each player rides a specially trained polo pony. Polo players usually play the game outdoors, although there are indoor polo matches, too. Three people play on each team in an indoor polo match.

The average polo field is 300 yards (275 m) long and 200 yards (182 m) wide. *Goal posts* are set up 24 yards (7.3 m) apart at each end of the field. A goal is scored when a player knocks the polo ball between the goal posts of the opposing team. The team with the most goals wins.

A polo ball is slightly over 3 inches (7.6 cm) in diameter. It is usually made of solid willow root and weighs a little more than 4 ounces (113 g). Polo players use long-handled mallets to hit the ball back and forth. They don't strike the ball with the end of the head of the mallet, as in croquet. Instead, the players hit the ball with the side of the mallet.

The periods in polo are called *chukkers*. Each chukker lasts for 7½ minutes. There are either six or eight chukkers in a polo match.

In the United States, the number of goals a polo player is expected to score in a game is called the player's handicap. The highest handicap anyone can have is ten. In a polo game, the handicaps of each team are added

▼ The earliest form of polo was played in Persia (now Iran) as a method of training cavalry troops for battle.

up. Then the smaller rating is subtracted from the higher rating. The difference is added to the weaker team's score.

The modern game of polo originated in India. Indian horsemen introduced the sport to British army officers. When the officers returned home to England, they organized polo matches there. Some wealthy American sportsmen saw polo matches in England in the 1870s. They liked the game and introduced it to the United States.

▶▶▶▶ **FIND OUT MORE** ◀◀◀◀
Sports

POLO, MARCO
(about 1254–1324)

The adventurer Marco Polo made an incredible journey—from Venice overland to China. He was the first to tell Europeans about the riches and the many unusual sights of the East.

◀ The modern game of polo requires exceptional riding skill, and ponies with stamina and courage.

▲ Marco Polo and his traveling companions were kindly received by Kublai Khan, who was interested in other countries.

His father and uncle were wealthy merchants. They had already made one trip to Cathay (now China), and on their second trip, they took the 17-year-old Marco with them. After a dangerous caravan trip lasting more than three years, they reached Khanbalik (now Beijing, China), the capital of the Mongol Empire. They stayed at the palace of the emperor, Kublai Khan. Marco became one of the emperor's closest friends. For the next 17 years, Marco Polo traveled all over the empire and even served for a while as governor of a Chinese city. He was amazed to find an advanced civilization in China that was superior to Europe's.

The Polos returned to Venice in 1295. Marco dictated a long and detailed account of what he had seen in Asia. His adventures soon became known throughout Europe.

Few people believed Marco's story, and he was called the greatest liar in history. Europeans could not believe that an advanced and cultured civilization existed in China. But in later years, people began to take a real interest in Marco Polo's careful observations. Mapmakers followed his descriptions, and explorers and traders, who set out to investigate for themselves, discovered his travel stories were accurate.

▼ Many of the thousands of Pacific Islands are of volcanic origin. The soil is fertile and supports many crops.

▶▶▶▶ **FIND OUT MORE** ◀◀◀◀
China; Exploration

POLYMER

SEE PLASTIC

POLYNESIA

Polynesia (meaning "many islands") is part of a large group of Pacific islands called Oceania. The other island groups of Oceania are Melanesia ("black islands") and Micronesia ("little islands"). The Polynesian islands are scattered over the central and southern Pacific. Most of the islands lie in small groups. The most important island groups are Samoa, Tonga, the Cook Islands, the Society Islands (including Tahiti), and the Marquesas Islands.

Many of the Polynesian islands were formed by ancient volcanoes. The volcanic islands are often rugged and mountainous. Rain clouds build up around the mountains, and the soil is usually rich and fertile. Other islands are low *atolls*. An atoll is a ring-shaped coral reef surrounding a lagoon, or shallow pond of water. A channel usually leads through the reef to the open sea. Most of these coral islands have poor soil, and the climate is dry.

The people of Polynesia are tall and graceful with light brown skins and black, wavy hair. Their language is related to the languages spoken in the other Pacific islands and in Southeast Asia. Many of the Polynesians are farmers. Coconuts are the only crop that grows well on the dry atolls. *Copra* (dried coconut meat from which coconut oil is made) is one of Polynesia's major exports. Farmers on the fertile volcanic islands grow crops such as yams and *taros* (root vegetables), bananas, sugarcane, cacao, pineapples, and vanilla. Most of the islanders have pigs and poultry.

POLYNESIA

Country or Territory	Status	Area in sq. mi	Area in sq. km	Population	Capital
American Samoa	U.S. territory	76	197	46,800	Fagatogo on Tutuila
Clipperton Island	French dependency	2	5	Uninhabited	——
Cook Islands	New Zealand territory	93	241	17,700	Avarua on Rarotonga
Easter Island	Chilean dependency	64	166	1,900	Hanga Roa
Gambler Islands*	French over-seas territory	36	93	582	Rikitea on Mangareva
Howland, Baker, and Jarvis Islands	U.S. possession	3	8	Uninhabited	——
Johnston Atoll	U.S. possession	1	2.5	1,327	——
Line Islands (Christmas, Palmyra, and other Islands**)	U.S. and British territory	164	425	2,300	——
Marquesas Islands*	French over-seas territory	491	1,271	7,500	Taishae on Nukuhiva
Midway Islands	U.S. territory	2	5	13	——
Niue Island	New Zealand territory	100	259	2,150	Aloft
Phoenix Islands (Canton, Enderbury, and other islands**)	U.S. and British territory	10	26	250	Nabari
Pitcairn Islands	British colony	2	5	61	Adamstown
Society Islands*	French over-seas territory	650	1,684	162,600	Papeete on Tahiti
Tonga	Independent (1970)	270	699	103,000	Nuku'alofa
Tuamotu Archipelago*	French over-seas territory	263	681	12,400	Apataki
Tubual or Austral Islands*	French over-seas territory	67	174	6,500	Mataura on Tubuai
Western Samoa	Independent (1962)	1,097	2,842	157,200	Apia
Wallis and Futura Islands	French over-seas territory	106	275	15,400	Mata-Utu on Wallis

*Part of French Polynesia
**Excluding islands belonging to Kiribati

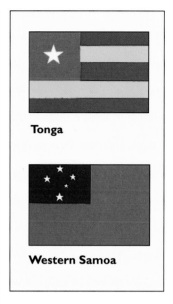

Tonga

Western Samoa

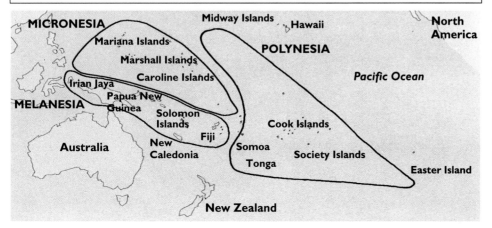

◄ The Polynesian Islands are scattered across the central Pacific. Midway Island marks the northern boundary, and New Zealand marks the southern. Easter Island is the island farthest to the east—4,000 miles (6,400 km) from New Zealand.

▲ These huge stone sculptures are on Easter Island. Nobody knows who made them. Today, some Polynesians live on Easter Island.

The Roman writer Pliny the Younger described what happened when Vesuvius destroyed Pompeii. According to Pliny, the ground shook, the sea sucked back and then hurled forward, and great tongues of flame spurted from the black cloud that boiled up from the volcano. Ashes fell and darkness closed in.

▶ When Mount Vesuvius erupted, the citizens of Pompeii were buried in ashes and molten lava. When this cooled and the bodies decomposed, molds of the bodies were left. Archeologists have poured plaster into the molds to make casts of the bodies of the victims.

The Polynesians are also expert sailors and fishermen. They build strong and graceful outrigger canoes. In the past, Polynesians made long ocean voyages. The Maoris sailed across the Pacific to settle in New Zealand. Some experts believe the Polynesians may originally have come from South America.

The islanders are famous for their crafts. Their traditional carved wooden war clubs and religious figures are now seen mainly in museums. But the people today are still skilled at weaving baskets from the leaves of the coconut palm.

Most Polynesians are now Christian. But their ceremonial dancing and singing, still practiced on many of the islands, shows that the old Polynesian religion is not completely forgotten. The idea of *tapu* (taboo)—that certain objects or people should not be touched—was an important part of this religion.

Easter Island in Polynesia holds one of the strangest mysteries in the Pacific. Gigantic stone heads stand on the cliffs of this island, looking out to sea. No one knows the age of the statues or who carved them.

The English explorer, Captain James Cook, visited the Polynesian islands in the 1700s. He found a people with a rich and well-organized way of life. But European traders and colonists, who flocked to Polynesia in the 1800s, brought diseases that killed large numbers of the islanders.

By the end of the century, most of the islands had been claimed by European countries or by the United States. Tonga and Western Samoa are independent island countries in Polynesia. Some of the Line and Phoenix islands in Polynesia are part of the independent island nation of Kiribati in Micronesia. Other Polynesian islands belong to, or are controlled by, France, Great Britain, Chile, New Zealand, and the United States.

Polynesians play an important part in local government on most of the islands. Visitors come from all over the world and tourism is bringing new wealth to Polynesia.

▶▶▶▶ **FIND OUT MORE** ◀◀◀◀
Cook, Captain James; Hawaii; Melanesia; Micronesia; New Zealand; Pacific Ocean

POMPEII

Pompeii was an ancient Roman city in southern Italy. It lay at the foot of the volcano Mount Vesuvius, on the beautiful coast of the Bay of Naples. Pompeii was a busy port and prosperous trading center. Several Roman nobles built large *villas*, or houses, near the city.

On the morning of August 24, A.D. 79, when the city was thronged with traders and visitors, Mount Vesuvius erupted. A black, suffocating cloud of ashes blanketed the whole area. Two days later, Pompeii and the nearby cities of Herculaneum and Stabiae lay buried under a deep layer of ashes and mud. About 2,000 people had died.

The cities remained buried, and as the years passed they were forgotten. In the 1700s, farmers digging in their land near Mount Vesuvius began to find traces of the ancient cities. Archeologists gradually discovered almost all of Pompeii. Much of the city was found exactly as it had been on the day of the eruption. Skeletons of the people who had died in the disaster lay covered in ashes that had

dried around them like plaster casts. A dog lay in one of the houses, still chained to his post. Meals, left hurriedly, still lay on the tables. The shops were filled with merchandise.

Visitors can now walk through the streets of Pompeii and into the temples, houses, and shops. They can read advertisements on the walls and admire the paintings and mosaics that decorate the houses. More than half of the city has been uncovered today. Pompeii tells a fascinating story about the ancient Romans.

▶ ▶ ▶ ▶ **FIND OUT MORE** ◀ ◀ ◀ ◀
Rome, Ancient; Volcano

PONCE DE LEON, JUAN (about 1460–1521)

Juan Ponce de León was one of the early explorers of the New World. He claimed the island of Puerto Rico and the land of Florida for his country, Spain.

Ponce de León was born in San Servas in the province of León, Spain. He first sailed to the New World with Christopher Columbus in 1493. Ponce de León conquered Boriquén (now Puerto Rico) in 1508 and became the first governor of the island.

The Caribs on Puerto Rico told Ponce de León about a rich land called Bimini, which lay to the north. They said that Bimini contained the legendary Fountain of Youth, a magical spring that would keep a person young forever. Ponce de León sailed from Puerto Rico in 1513. His aim, according to legend, was to find the Fountain of Youth. On Easter, he reached a land of beautiful flowers that he named *La Florida*. The Spanish word for flower is *florida*. He explored much of the coast of Florida and then returned to Puerto Rico.

Ponce de León returned to Florida in 1521 to set up a colony. But he was wounded in a battle with local Native Americans. He was taken to the island of Cuba, where he died.

▶ ▶ ▶ **FIND OUT MORE** ◀ ◀ ◀
Exploration; Florida;
Puerto Rico

POND LIFE

A small, still pond may look like a very quiet place. But if you look carefully, you will see that it is filled with plenty of activity.

Many different kinds of plants and animals live in ponds. The mass of green scum you may have seen floating on a pond is really a huge colony of tiny, threadlike plants called *spirogyra*. These plants are part of the algae group. If you look at a drop of pond water under a microscope, you may see a number of tiny creatures. Some of them may move very fast, and others scarcely move at all. These single-celled animals are called *protozoa*. Protozoa, along with tiny worms and other small animals called *crustaceans*, serve as food for fish and other water creatures.

Yellow perch, bass, pickerel, bream, and brook trout are common

◀ The intense heat during the destruction of Pompeii helped save objects not usually found by archeologists. Bread, seeds, and nuts, for example, were burned to carbon and preserved.

▼ Ponce de León's route when he set out to discover the mythical Fountain of Youth. This expedition led to the eventual settling of Florida by the Spanish.

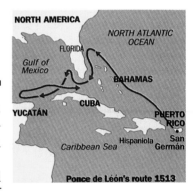

◀ Ponce de León, Spanish explorer of Florida.

◀ A net and a tray are all you need to study the animals that live in a pond. Make sure to keep away from deep water and steep banks.

▶ Ponds are often rich in nutrients and have plentiful plant life, which provides food for insects and other small creatures.

around the water, a number of different kinds of water plants may grow. Besides providing food and oxygen, these plants offer protection and nesting places for other forms of

pond fish. Freshwater clams, crayfish, snails, frogs, and water snakes are also found in many ponds. Some ponds contain *leeches*, creatures that can cling to a body and suck blood. Leeches often attach themselves to the turtles that crawl and swim in ponds. Many forms of young and adult insects also live in and around ponds. Mosquitoes and dragonflies fly over ponds. Water beetles, mayflies, and other insects skim across pond surfaces.

On some pond surfaces, there may be water lilies and water lily pads (leaves), which are rooted at the bottom of the pond. Underneath and

pond life.

In winter, when the water freezes, many pond creatures hibernate by burying themselves in the mud at the bottom of the pond.

Many birds like to visit ponds to look for food or just to swim. Ducks, swans, and geese are often seen in ponds. Herons and other fish-eating birds will come to a pond for food. Small mammals, such as beavers and otters, live near ponds. Beavers store their winter food in the dams they build in ponds.

▼ Many creatures are found living in and around ponds.
1. Dragonfly 2. Whirligig beetle 3. Pintail 4. Frog
5. Pond skater 6. Caddis fly
7. Frog spawn 8. Water beetle 9. Mosquito larvae
10. Pond snail 11. Common newt 12. Crested newt
13. Diving beetle 14. Tadpoles
15. Stickleback 16. Diving beetle's air bubble 17. Water spider 18. Water boatman
19. Snail eggs 20. Ramshorn snail

▶ ▶ ▶ ▶ **FIND OUT MORE** ◀ ◀ ◀ ◀
Algae; Animal Distribution; Animal Homes; Beaver; Bird; Clams and Oysters; Crustacean; Dragonfly; Ducks and Geese; Fish; Food Web; Frogs and Toads; Insect; Mosquito; Plant Distribution; Protozoan; Snails and Slugs; Snake; Turtle

PONTIAC (about 1720–1769)

Pontiac was a chief of the Ottawa tribe who made a brave effort to stop English settlement in the regions of Indiana, Ohio, and Illinois. He secretly organized an alliance of almost all the Native American tribes

from Lake Superior to the Gulf of Mexico. He also allied himself with the French.

At that time, France and England were fighting to see which country would gain control of North America. Pontiac arranged to have his warriors attack English forts in different places throughout the frontier on a certain day, in May 1763. Pontiac led an attack on the British fort at Detroit. There, he fought the British for six months. By that time, however, the French had lost the French and Indian War.

Without French support, Pontiac was helpless against the British army. The alliance of tribes came to an end. Pontiac finally agreed to a peace treaty with the British in 1765.

▶▶▶▶ **FIND OUT MORE** ◀◀◀◀
French and Indian Wars

PONY

SEE HORSE

galloped on horseback across the frontier with mail sacks strapped to their saddles. Some of the riders were killed or wounded by Native American arrows or bullets. But only one sack of mail was ever lost by the Pony Express.

The Pony Express began carrying mail between St. Joseph, Missouri, and San Francisco, California, on April 3, 1860. Riders carried the mail about 1,900 miles (3,050 km) from St. Joseph to Sacramento, California. Relay stations were set up about every 10 to 15 miles (15 to 25 km) along the way. There they could change to fresh horses. Each rider rode about 75 miles (120 km) every day. At Sacramento, the mail was loaded onto boats to be taken to San Francisco.

The Pony Express route was a dangerous one. In addition to hostile Native Americans and bandits, riders were sometimes slowed down by snowstorms, sandstorms, and floods.

The first Pony Express trip took about 10½ days. Later trips averaged between 8 to 10 days. This was less

▲ Pontiac, a Native American chief, confers with the council of his tribe.

PONY EXPRESS

The "Pony Express" was the name given to the mail service that operated between Missouri and California from 1860 to 1861. Mail carriers

than half as long as stagecoach mail delivery took. The fastest time ever made by Pony Express riders was 7 days and 17 hours, to deliver copies of President Lincoln's inaugural address in 1861.

▲ A Pony Express rider changes horses at one of the many staging posts along the route from Missouri to California.

▲ A statue of Saint Peter, the first pope.

The Pony Express was founded by a freight company. The company first charged five dollars for carrying each half ounce of mail, but this price was later reduced to one dollar. "Buffalo Bill" Cody, "Wild Bill" Hickok, and "Pony Bob" Haslam were among the tough and wiry Pony Express riders.

The Pony Express lasted for only about 18 months. The first coast-to-coast telegraph line was completed on October 22, 1861. This made it possible for people to flash messages across the nation in minutes. Two days after the telegraph began, the Pony Express made its last trip.

▶▶▶▶ **FIND OUT MORE** ◀◀◀◀
Buffalo Bill; Hickok, Wild Bill; Postal Service

POPE

The pope is head of the Roman Catholic Church. The word *pope* comes from the Latin word *papa,* which means "father." The pope has several other titles, including Bishop of Rome and Supreme Pontiff of the Universal Church. The pope is usually called by a first, or Christian, name that he chooses when he

becomes pope. The office of pope is called the *papacy.* The pope lives in Vatican City, an independent state within Rome, Italy.

The pope is elected by a group of Roman Catholic bishops called *cardinals.* When a pope dies, cardinals from all over the world travel to Vatican City. A sacred *conclave* (meeting) begins from 15 to 18 days after the pope's death. The cardinals are locked inside the Vatican palace until they have chosen a new pope. The voting is conducted in secret in the Sistine Chapel. In order for a candidate to be elected pope, he must receive two-thirds plus one of the ballots cast. Any adult Roman Catholic man can be elected pope, but ever since the 1300s, every pope has been a cardinal.

The pope lives in the Vatican palace. During the summer, he may reside at Castel Gandolfo near Rome. The pope receives no salary. The Church supplies him with all his needs.

The pope has many duties. With the bishops of the world, he makes decisions and rulings about moral and religious matters affecting Roman Catholics. The pope is also the ruler of Vatican City. At one time, the popes ruled a large area of land in

▲ Pope Gregory I, called the Great, did much to spread Christianity throughout the world.

▶ Pope Sixtus IV, shown with four of his nephews, one of whom later became Pope Julius II.

2128

Italy called the Papal States. In 1870, the papal states were seized by the newly formed kingdom of Italy. In 1929, Italy and the Vatican signed a treaty, and Vatican City became an independent state.

History of the Popes

In the early years of Christianity, Rome was the capital city of the Roman Empire. Saint Peter, the apostle of Jesus Christ, was the first bishop of the Christian Church in Rome. As written in the Bible, Jesus Christ said to Peter (whose name means "rock"), "Thou art Peter, and upon this rock I shall build my Church." Roman Catholics believe that Christ intended for Peter to be the first head of the Christian Church. After Christ's death and resurrection, Peter soon left Jerusalem for Rome. Since that time, Rome has been the traditional home of the popes.

More than 260 popes have ruled the Church since Saint Peter's time. Many have been great men. In the A.D. 400s, Leo I twice saved Rome from destruction by savage invaders. Pope Gregory XIII, in the 1500s, established the Gregorian Calendar, which is still in use today. Pope Leo XIII, in the late 1800s, spoke out in support of the working people and labor unions.

Popes in recent times have encouraged a closer understanding among various Christian churches. Pope John XXIII spoke out strongly against suffering and war. He welcomed leaders of other faiths to visit him. He was much admired throughout the world. John organized the Second Vatican Council, which met several times to find ways of modernizing the church. The council started some of the greatest changes the church has experienced in the last 400 years. After the death of John XXIII, Paul VI was elected in 1963. He was the first pope to travel to many countries, and he was the first

to visit the Holy Land, the United States, and South America. He died in 1978, as did his successor, Pope John Paul I, who served only 34 days. Cardinal Karol Wojtyla of Poland was then chosen pope and took the name John Paul II. He became the first non-Italian pope since 1523. He, too, has traveled more widely than any previous pope.

▶▶▶▶ **FIND OUT MORE** ◀◀◀◀

Christianity; Italian History; Protestant Reformation; Religion; Roman Catholic Church; Vatican City

◀ **Pope John Paul II, the first Polish pope. He has won the affection of people throughout the world with his humble act of kissing the ground when visiting abroad.**

There have been 23 popes called John. The first was pope from A.D. 523 to 526. John XXIII was pope from 1958 to 1963.

 ## POPULAR MUSIC

Music that many people like to listen to is called popular ("pop") music. It is the music played on jukeboxes, by disc jockeys on radios, and on pop videos. It is the "hit" that nobody had heard of yesterday, but that everybody is listening to today. By the end of the month, a new record will have replaced it in popularity. Few people can predict which pop songs will become popular. Publicity helps produce a hit song or star singers. But the music must communicate some emotion or feeling to the listeners, and singers must have some quality of voice, appearance, or personality that reaches out to people.

▲ Elvis Presley brought rock 'n' roll music alive for hundreds of people. He still has a thriving fan-club today.

▼ The Beatles–(from left to right) Ringo Starr, Paul McCartney, George Harrison, and John Lennon. All four members were born in Liverpool, England. They became the most popular group in rock history.

Popular music has always been a part of life in the United States. The early settlers sang tunes that were popular in Europe, but soon people began putting new words to the old tunes. "Yankee Doodle," which has been called America's first popular song, was a great favorite of the colonial soldiers fighting in the Revolutionary War.

"The Star-Spangled Banner," with its patriotic words written by Francis Scott Key, was sung to a familiar tune of that time. It quickly became a popular song and was sung in the theaters, taverns, and homes. It was not long before it was adopted by the U.S. Army and Navy. President Woodrow Wilson formally declared it to be the U.S. national anthem in 1916, but Congress did not vote on it until 1931.

During the late 1800s, U.S. popular music included patriotic songs, love ballads, minstrel and vaudeville songs, and the blues or work-songs of black musicians. Stephen Foster and Daniel Emmett were popular songwriters of that time.

By the early 1900s, many publishers of popular music had their offices on 28th Street in New York City. Songwriters were kept busy composing melodies on pianos. Their instruments were not always in good tune, and many songwriters tried to quiet the sound by laying newspapers between the piano strings. Someone

once remarked that these muffled pianos sounded like tin pans, and the whole street sounded like a "tin pan alley." This became the name for the popular music business.

Every music publisher sent "song pluggers" out to popularize their songs by singing them in restaurants and bars and convincing popular entertainers to use them. Pianists were hired by music stores to play the printed music so that customers could hear it. Popular songs in the early 1900s included ragtime and jazz rhythm pieces, as well as songs from operettas and other stage performances. The invention of the phonograph, radio, and the talking movies brought music to more and more people and was important in making songs popular.

From the 1920s to about 1950, there were three main kinds of popular music: the music of dance bands and the songs from Tin Pan Alley; black popular music, often called rhythm and blues; and country-and-western music. The songs from musical comedies and movies were also growing in popularity.

In the 1950s, rock 'n' roll became the most important popular music. It developed from mixing rhythm and blues and country-and-western music with the regular popular music style. Elvis Presley was the first, and perhaps greatest, star of rock 'n' roll music. The rock-and-roll beat spread from Memphis and Detroit throughout the world. Four young musicians (Ringo Starr, Paul McCartney, George Harrison, and John Lennon) from Liverpool, England, called themselves "The Beatles" and became very popular and successful in the 1960s and 1970s.

Most rock music is played on electronic instruments, and is amplified to make it very loud and to add special sound effects. Lasers and flashing lights are used to create exciting effects on live performances, but most pop music is recorded in the

controlled conditions of the studio. Much of today's popular music is a mixture of several musical styles, including rock 'n' roll, country-and-western, and folk.

▶▶▶▶ FIND OUT MORE ◀◀◀◀

Dylan, Bob; Electronic Music; Folk Song; Foster, Stephen; Jazz; Music; Musical Comedy; Musical Instruments; Opera; Presley, Elvis; Recording; Star-Spangled Banner; Vaudeville

POPULATION

The total number of people who live in an area make up its *population*. The word comes from the Latin word for "people." To plan for the future, governments of cities and countries need to know how many persons they govern. Nearly all countries of the world regularly count the number of people living in them. This population count is called a *census*. Most countries take a census every ten years. The United States took its last census in 1990. Highly developed, industrialized countries can provide accurate figures. Underdeveloped and undeveloped countries

UNITED STATES POPULATION GROWTH
1620 TO 1990, AND PROJECTED TO 2010

1620	2,500*	1880	50,155,783
1700	275,000*	1890	62,947,714
1740	890,000*	1900	75,994,575
1750	1,207,000*	1910	91,972,266
1760	1,610,000*	1920	105,710,620
1770	2,205,000*	1930	122,775,046
1780	2,781,000*	1940	131,669,275
1790	3,929,214	1950	151,325,798
1800	5,308,483	1960	179,323,175
1810	7,239,881	1970	203,235,298
1820	9,638,453	1980	226,504,825
1830	12,866,020	1990	248,709,873
1840	17,069,453	——	——
1850	23,191,876	2000	c. 260,378,000
1860	32,443,321	2010	c. 280,000,000
1870	39,818,449		

WORLD POPULATION GROWTH
10,000 B.C. TO 1990, AND PROJECTED TO 2000

10,000 B.C.	10,000,000	1850	1,130,000,000
A.D. 1	300,000,000	1900	1,600,000,000
1600	500,000,000	1950	2,510,000,000
1700	625,000,000	1990	5,300,000,000
1800	910,000,000	2000	c. 6,200,000,000

* estimated colonial population
c. approximate figure

▼ This map shows the most densely populated areas of the world.

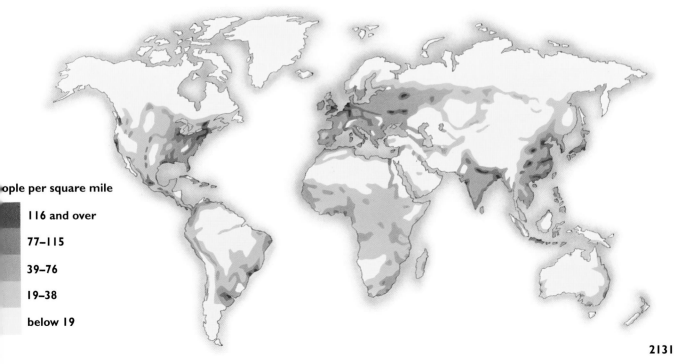

ople per square mile

116 and over

77–115

39–76

19–38

below 19

> The population of western Europe is decreasing quite rapidly. It has been calculated that there will be 25 million fewer people in western Europe by the year 2050, if the present birth rate continues.

Oceania
26 million

North and
Central America
420 million

Asia
3100 million

South America
290 million

Europe (inc. Russia)
646 million

Africa
795 million

▲ The world's population is distributed very unevenly. Asia has the most people, and the total population of China and India add up to more than 40 percent of all the world's people.

▶ The Canadian porcupine is a tree-living species. It feeds on bark and buds. The short, spiny tail is used as a weapon.

may produce less accurate population figures.

A census tells more than just the number of people living in a particular place. The census asks people certain questions, such as how much money they make, where they live, and whether they own or rent their homes. Census figures can be understood only when a person knows how they were determined. The population of a city can vary greatly, depending on whether the number of people in the central city, or in the entire *metropolitan* (urban) area are counted. For example, according to the U.S. 1990 census, 574,283 people lived in the central city of Boston. But 2,871,000 people lived in Boston's metropolitan area.

This encyclopedia includes population figures put together by the United Nations. The estimated population of the world is now more than five billion people, according to the United Nations. More than half of these people live in Asia. The world's population is now growing faster than ever before in history. Many hundreds of years passed before it reached one billion people in 1840. Only 90 years later, in 1930, it had grown to two billion people. That number doubled again by 1975. Scientists predict that by the year 2000, the Earth will have more than ten billion people. Such rapid population growth is called a *population explosion.*

Will there be enough food to feed everybody? Some scientists are worried that there will not be. Why are

there so many more people? One reason is that people now know much more about health care. People live longer, and fewer die of disease. Many more babies now live to become adults.

Population figures change because of *migration.* Migration is a shift in population caused by people moving from one place to another. The U.S. 1990 census showed that the fastest growing states in population are in the South and Southwest. Many people have also left the larger northern cities. And more Americans are living in the *suburbs,* areas surrounding cities, or in rural areas.

Some people believe that the population must be kept from growing any more. They urge parents to have no more than two children. This way, the children would simply replace their parents, and population growth would stop. This idea is often referred to as *zero population growth,* or ZPG.

▶▶▶▶ **FIND OUT MORE** ◀◀◀◀
Immigration

PORCELAIN

SEE POTTERY AND CHINA

PORCUPINE

Porcupines are animals that are covered with sharp *quills,* which are very

stiff hairs. They are rodents and have large front teeth like their relatives, the squirrel and the rat. Porcupines are divided into two main groups: Old World porcupines and New World porcupines. Old World porcupines live in the forests and grasslands of Europe, Africa, and Asia. They can run fast, but they cannot climb trees. New World porcupines live in forests in North and South America. They are slow moving, but are good tree climbers. Both types of porcupines are plant-eaters. They mate in the fall, and the female usually bears one young in the spring.

A porcupine's quills grow out of its back, sides, and tail. When a porcupine becomes angry, it raises its quills and moves backward toward its enemy. The quills can become painfully embedded in the enemy's flesh and are very difficult to pull out because they have hooked ends. It is not true that porcupines can shoot their quills like spears. A porcupine's quills come out very easily, especially when the animal shakes its body.

The Canadian porcupine is a common New World porcupine. It grows about 30 inches (76 cm) long and has brownish hair. Porcupines that live in Central and South America have long, thin tails like monkeys. They use their tails to hold onto the branches of the trees they live in.

►►►► **FIND OUT MORE** ◄◄◄◄
Animal; Animal Defenses; Rodent

PORPOISE

SEE DOLPHINS AND PORPOISES

PORTER, WILLIAM

SEE HENRY, O.

▲ ***Sir Thomas More*, by Hans Holbein the Younger, a portrait painted in 1527.**

PORTRAIT

A portrait is a work of art showing us how a person looks. It is usually a painting, but sculptors and photographers also do portraits. If the person creating the portrait is a true artist, he or she shows us not only how the *subject* (person being portrayed) looks, but also something about the subject—what the person's occupation, life style, or character is.

Many ancient cultures—the Egyptians, the Greeks, and the Romans, for example—used portraits. The artists often did not flatter their subjects, because they wanted to show the real character of a Roman emperor in his *bust* (sculptured head). Medieval people cared less about portraits, but by 1500, they were fashionable again.

Here is a portrait of Sir Thomas More, an English official of the early

▶ *Eva Gonzales*, by the French artist Edouard Manet. He has used her dress as a contrast to the dark background of the painting, leaving everything else in shadow.

1500s. With the chain of his office (as Chancellor of England) around his neck, he looks like a person who has great decisions to make. The folded paper in his hand is probably some order that he has just written.

The More portrait is a *posed* one—which means the artist has portrayed the subject sitting very still. The artist has also given great attention to the fur and the velvet of the clothing, and has taken great care with all the details. There are no strong shadows. Everything is lighted. Later, portrait painters often attempted to show their subjects as if caught in action. Thomas Eakins, an American of about 100 years ago, would paint a surgeon operating, or a man pausing to think about what has just been said. To concentrate attention more on the subject, such a painter might put the head in strong light.

Look at the pictures of people in this book. How do they differ?

▶▶▶▶ **FIND OUT MORE** ◀◀◀◀
Dutch and Flemish Art; Gainsborough, Thomas; Hals, Frans; Holbein the Younger; Leonardo da Vinci; Rembrandt van Rijn; Reynolds, Joshua; Roman Art; Rubens, Peter Paul; Rushmore, Mount; Sculpture; Titian; Toulouse-Lautrec, Henri de; Velázquez, Diego

▲ The Portuguese are a seafaring people for whom fishing is an important activity. Here, a fisherman mends his nets on the shore.

PORTUGAL

The small country of Portugal was once the center of a powerful and wealthy empire. Adventurous Portuguese explored the seas and established colonies in America, Asia, and Africa. Prince Henry the Navigator studied charts and started Portuguese seafarers on voyages of discovery in the 1400s. The work of Prince Henry's sea captains and their successors led to a planned system of exploration. Bartholomeu Dias, the first to sail around the Cape of Good Hope; Vasco da Gama, who discovered a sea route to Asia; and Ferdinand Magellan, the first to circle the globe, were some of the explorers. Portuguese ships brought home the treasures of distant lands. In the 1700s and 1800s, Portugal's empire included colonies in Africa, Asia, and South America. Today, these colonies are independent nations. Portugal has one remaining overseas territory, the tiny enclave of Macao on China's south coast. Macao will be returned to China in 1999.

Portugal is the westernmost country of continental Europe. It is located on the western part of the Iberian Peninsula, which it shares with Spain. Spain borders Portugal on the north and east, and the Atlantic Ocean borders it on the south and west. Portugal includes two island groups in the North Atlantic: the Azores and the Madeiras. (See the map with the article on SPAIN.)

The Portuguese have always turned to the sea for food and transportation. Portugal has about 400 miles (650 km) of coast along the Atlantic. Important ports and many small fishing villages lie on this coast. Fishermen go out into the Atlantic Ocean in small boats to catch cod, sardines, and anchovies.

The largest port is Lisbon, the capital city. It lies on the north bank of the mouth of the Tagus River. A Moorish castle, built in the 900s, over-

looks the old part of the town, where streets are narrow and winding. Some streets are so steep that people ride up and down in cable cars. Lisbon was rebuilt following an earthquake in 1755 that killed many people and almost destroyed the city.

The land north of the Tagus is mountainous. Dark forests of pine and oak cover the rocky hills. Rivers have cut deep valleys into the mountains. Porto (or Oporto), Portugal's second largest city, lies along the Douro River. The hills around Porto produce grapes that are made into port wine. Coimbra is Portugal's university city. Portuguese industry produces textiles, metal products, paper, and electronic equipment.

Rolling plains lie south of the Tagus River. Olive trees and cork oaks grow here. Portugal is the largest cork producer in the world. The cork grows as bark on these oaks. Workers peel the bark off the oaks in long strips. The plains also produce wheat, rye, and citrus fruits. Farmers work the small lots with oxen and mules.

The Algarve, a resort section of beautiful beaches on the southern coast, is enjoyed by many tourists. The city of Estoril near Lisbon is also a beach resort. Entertainers in cafes often sing the *fado*, a song that tells a sad story. The people of Portugal work hard, but they also celebrate festivals with parades and fireworks.

The Portuguese are descended from the Lusitanians, Romans, and Arabs who in turn ruled the land. In the 1100s, Portugal became an independent kingdom. Before that time, its history was tied with that of Spain as a part of the Iberian Peninsula. The Portuguese language is spoken by more than 145 million people in various parts of the world.

Since 1910, Portugal has been a republic. For more than 30 years, however, the people lived under the dictatorial rule of Antonio Salazar. The Portuguese had few rights then. Salazar's secret police crushed all political opposition. In 1968, Salazar suffered a stroke, and he died two years later. Marcelo Caetano, Portugal's new ruler, was less of a dictator.

In 1974, a leftist military group overthrew Caetano and made many reforms. The secret police was abolished, and rights were restored to the people. Political parties were allowed in the country. Free elections have been held in Portugal since 1976. In 1986, the country became a member of the European Community.

▶▶▶▶ **FIND OUT MORE** ◀◀◀◀
Brazil; Dias, Bartholomeu; Gama, Vasco da; Macao; Magellan, Ferdinand

PORTUGAL

Capital city
Lisbon
(830,000 people)

Area
35,553 square miles
(92,080 sq. km)

Population
10,434,000 people

Government
Republic

Natural resources
Tungsten, iron ore, uranium ore, marble, coal, copper

Export products
Cotton, textiles, cork and cork products, canned fish, wine, timber, resin, machinery and transport equipment, paper, footwear

Unit of money
Escudo

Official language
Portuguese

Minho R.
Vinha R.
Viana do Castelo
Bragança
Tâmega R.
Braga
Guimarães
Vila Real
Porto
Douro R.
ATLANTIC OCEAN
Aveiro
Viseu
Mondego R.
Guarda
Estrela ▲ 6,539 ft. 1,993 m.
Coimbra
Cape Mondego
Covilhã
Zêzere R.
Castelo Branco
Leiria
Cape Carvoeiro
Sor R.
Santarém
Tagus R.
Portalegre
Seda R.
Sorraia R.
Lisbon
Almada
Barreiro
Évora
Setúbal
Cape Espichel
Setúbal Bay
Sado R.
Beja
Guadiana R.
Portimão
Cape St. Vincent
Faro
Gulf of Cadiz

0   50   100 Miles
0   50   100   150 Kilometers
© 1994 GeoSystems, an R.R. Donnelley & Sons Company

▲ This is the world's first *adhesive* ("stick-on") postage stamp: the British penny black of 1840.

▲ Mailboxes, also called collection boxes, can be found in every U.S. town.

There was a postal service in ancient Persia in 500 B.C., where runners carried messages for the king and government officials. The Greek historian Herodotus wrote: "Neither snow nor rain nor heat nor gloom of night stays these couriers from the swift completion of their appointed rounds." These words can be seen today, carved above the entrance to the General Post Office in New York City.

PORTUGUESE

SEE ROMANCE LANGUAGES

POSTAL SERVICE

When you mail a letter or a package, it goes on a very complicated journey. It starts with the mail carrier who collects your letter from the mailbox, and ends with the mail carrier who delivers it.

Types of Mail
The United States Postal Service divides mail into four classes. *First-class* mail includes letters, postcards, and sealed correspondence that is at least partly in writing. *Second-class* mail includes newspapers and magazines. *Third-class* mail includes printed material and packages that weigh less than a pound. *Fourth-class* mail (also called *parcel post)* is for packages that weigh more than a pound.

At the post office, all mail is bundled or placed in special trays and then packed in mailbags. Most mail is transported by truck or airplane. A few trains and ships carry mail. Almost all first-class mail going more than 100 miles (161 km) is carried by airplane. If you want your letter to arrive very quickly, you send it by *express mail.* Often it will be delivered to its exact destination the next day. If you send it by *special delivery,* it will be sent as quickly as possible.

You can also send a letter by *certified mail.* The receiver signs a receipt for your letter, and the receipt is sent back to you. This "certifies" that the letter was received, and by the proper person. *Registered mail* also uses the receipt system, but it is carried under special protection. Registered mail is most often used when mailing money (checks) or very valuable items.

All mail must be marked clearly with both the sender's and receiver's address. The ZIP Code number is very important. By reading the ZIP Code number, post office workers sort letters and get them to their destinations quickly. All mail must include the correct amount of postage (usually in stamps). Special instructions (such as "special delivery") must be written on the envelope or wrapper.

Postage
Postage is usually attached to mail as stamps that you can buy at a post office or from automatic stamp machines in some stores. Stamps have different values, and special stamps are printed for overseas airmail and special delivery. The U.S. Postal Service sells many special-issue stamps every year. These stamps are printed to honor particular people or events. Many people collect these unique stamps as a hobby.

You can buy postcards and envelopes with the postage already printed on them. Large companies with much correspondence use *postage meters* to stamp and cancel their own mail. A company must get a special permit to use a postage meter. Businesses that send out a great number of identical items, such as catalogs or newsletters, all on the same day may pay an annual fee for a bulk-rate permit stamp.

Handling of Mail
After you drop a letter into the mailbox, postal workers collect it and take it by truck to the post office in your area. Along *rural routes* (postal routes out in the country), the postal officials may pick up outgoing mail from your mailbox and place that day's mail back into the box. At the post office, the mail is first sorted according to class and size and whether it requires special handling. The mail is then *canceled.* Stamps are marked so they cannot be reused, and the *postmark* (post office name and date) is stamped on the envelope.

Next, the mail is sorted by desti-

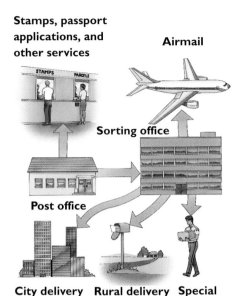

Stamps, passport applications, and other services

Airmail

Sorting office

Post office

City delivery   Rural delivery   Special delivery

nation. This is where the ZIP Code speeds things up. ZIP Code numbers indicate the post offices to which a letter must travel in order to reach its destination. The first numeral of a ZIP Code number tells you the *regional post office*. The next two numbers tell you the *city* or *county post office*. The last two numbers tell you the *zone*, or local area within a city or county. The ZIP Code number 60614 immediately tells a postal worker that the letter will go to the Chicago Regional Post Office (6), the post office of the city of Chicago (06), zone 14.

Big-city post offices have machines that can automatically cancel and sort letters according to ZIP Code. In smaller post offices, much of the canceling and sorting is done by hand.

Some people rent post office boxes. These boxes are located in a post office building. Each is numbered and mail is delivered there. Travelers often have their mail sent to *general delivery* at a post office in a particular city. The post office holds the mail until the traveler comes to pick it up. Letters without stamps or without enough postage will not be delivered and will be returned to the sender. Also, if the mail is

addressed incorrectly or if the receiver cannot be found, the mail is returned to the sender. If the receiver has moved and left a *forwarding address,* the mail is sent on to the new address. If the address of the sender was not included, mail cannot be returned and it goes to the *dead-letter office* where it is either sold or destroyed. Dead-letter packages are sold at public auction every few years.

History of Postal Systems

Postal systems first began as messenger services. One messenger would start out, run a certain distance, and give the letter to a second messenger. The second person would run to a third messenger, and so on. The Ancient Assyrians, Persians, Greeks, and Romans all had such systems.

The Romans later set up offices and inns along post roads where messengers could rest and get fresh horses. These places were marked by special posts at the roadside. The name "post office" comes from these early stations."

During the Middle Ages, postal systems were patterned from the Roman model. When Marco Polo traveled to China in the 1200s, he discovered that the Chinese had a very advanced postal system. As trade in Europe increased, people needed regular, scheduled messenger services. Post offices were set up in towns and people brought their letters in to be mailed. They paid the postmasters a fee, and the postmasters wrote their names on the envelopes to show that postage was paid.

◄ From collection to delivery, the U.S. Postal Service handles more than 150 billion pieces of mail each year.

▲ These local stamps were issued in the U.S. between 1840 and 1866 in competition with the official post office. They bear the name of the company issuing them.

▼ Letters can be sorted by using optical character reading devices. The letters pass by a sensor that picks up the characters of the ZIP Code.

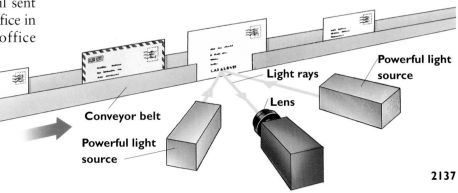

Powerful light source

Light rays

Lens

Conveyor belt

Powerful light source

Balloon mail floated over the heads of German soldiers during the siege of Paris in 1870–1871, keeping the city in touch with the rest of France. The first balloon mail stamp was issued in Tennessee in 1877.

In 1840, the British government began issuing postage stamps. To mail a letter, people bought stamps in advance and stuck them on their letters in place of the postmaster's signature.

The first post office in the United States was established in Boston in 1639. A man named Richard Fairbanks was given permission to set up a post office in his house. All letters to Boston were sent to the Fairbanks house where Bostonians came to pick up and send out mail. For every letter he received or delivered, Mr. Fairbanks got one penny. In 1691, the first American postal service was set up by Andrew Hamilton. Letters were carried by mail carriers on horseback between Boston, New York, Philadelphia, and Virginia.

In 1775, the Continental Congress established the first U.S. government postal system. Benjamin Franklin was appointed postmaster general.

International Mail

The Universal Postal Union is an organization of the United Nations that regulates mail service between countries. It has representatives from about 150 countries who set up rules concerning international postage rates, delivery procedures, and weights and sizes of international mail. The Union helps new nations set up postal systems, and it handles money matters that arise from international postage rates and services.

▶▶▶▶ **FIND OUT MORE** ◀◀◀◀
Franklin, Benjamin; Pony Express; United Nations

LEARN BY DOING

You can test your normal standing posture by standing against a wall in your usual position. Your shoulder blades and buttocks should both touch the wall. If they do not, your posture may need a small amount of correction. But do not worry too much. Ask your gym teacher at school, or your family doctor, to teach you some exercises that will help to strengthen your muscles and improve your posture.

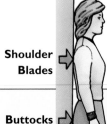

Shoulder Blades

Buttocks

 POSTURE

As you sit reading this article, you are probably not thinking about your *posture*, or the position of your body. But it is important to develop good posture control without even having to think about it.

Good posture refers to the way a normal, healthy person stands, sits, and moves. Posture cannot be defined in an exact way. It is the result of good physical and mental health. A person with good posture will usually stand with the head held high and the body held comfortably straight, but not rigid.

A good sitting position is one in which the back is held comfortably straight. It is easier to sit in a good position in a chair that is at a comfortable level, so that both feet can rest on the floor.

Most people develop their posture during childhood. Physical or emotional problems during this period can cause poor posture. For example, a person who cannot see well may develop the habit of thrusting the head forward to see better. Eventually, he or she will always stand or sit with the head pushed forward.

▶▶▶▶ **FIND OUT MORE** ◀◀◀◀
Exercise; Health

 POTATO

The potato is the world's most popular vegetable. It grows in a wide variety of soils and climates. It provides many nutritional needs, such as protein, calcium, and vitamin C.

Potato plants grow to be 3 to 4 feet (90–120 cm) tall. The edible parts, called *tubers*, grow from the stems underground. Most potato plants have about 4 of 5 tubers, but special varieties have as many as 20.

Potato plants live for only one growing season. New plants grow from mature tubers. You can see sprouts coming from the "eyes" of old potatoes.

People eat some form of potatoes at most main meals. Potato chips are popular snacks. The potato is also used to make flour and some types of starch.

Potatoes were first grown in South America. The Inca Indian civilization's unit of time was the time it took to cook a potato! The Spanish brought potatoes back to Europe in the 1500s. Europeans took potatoes to other parts of the world, including North America.

▶▶▶▶ **FIND OUT MORE** ◀◀◀◀
Inca; Vegetable

POTTER, BEATRIX (1866–1943)

Beatrix Potter was the author of *The Tale of Peter Rabbit.* The story began in the 1890s in letters to the sick child of a friend. When Potter started publishing her stories, she illustrated them herself with delicate drawings in soft, pale colors.

Beatrix Potter was born in London, England, and was educated by a governess. She had a pet rabbit, which was later the inspiration for the story about Peter Rabbit. Several generations of children have been delighted by the story of the adventurous rabbit named Peter that broke into Mr. MacGregor's cabbage patch and barely managed to get home with all his fur. Beatrix Potter also wrote other favorite stories, such as *The Tale*

of *Jemima Puddle-Duck, The Tale of Mr. Jeremy Fisher (a frog), The Tale of Two Bad Mice,* and *The Tale of Benjamin Bunny.*

If you check one of these books out of your school library, you may find that you enjoy it as much as your parents and grandparents did! Beatrix Potter loved small animals and lovely scenery and enjoyed drawing them. Over the years, her charming, humorous little tales have become familiar throughout most of the world. Beatrix Potter's stories have been translated into many languages. They have even been made into a ballet, created by the British Royal Ballet Company, and filmed as a movie.

▶▶▶▶ **FIND OUT MORE** ◀◀◀◀
Children's literature

POTTERY AND CHINA

Objects made from baked clay are called *ceramics.* The pottery maker, or *potter,* mixes clay with water to make it soft. Next he or she shapes the clay into an object. The potter *fires* the clay by putting it in very high heat. Firing changes the clay, making it stiff and hard. If you put water in an unfired pot, the clay will become soft and the pot will lose its shape.

Kinds of Ceramics
Ceramics made of fired clay are called *earthenware.* In ancient times, earthenware was fired by baking the shaped clay over hot coals for a long time. Today, earthenware is usually fired in a special oven, called a *kiln,* that can produce very high temperatures. Fired earthenware is *porous*— full of holes, called pores. These pores allow liquids to leak slowly through the fired clay. To keep it from leaking, earthenware is usually *glazed* (covered with a thin layer of glass). Glazes can be of different col-

▲ The potato plant stores its food as starch in special underground stems called *tubers.* This is the part of the plant that we eat.

◀ The British writer Beatrix Potter was also a talented illustrator. The pictures of Jemima Puddle-Duck (above) and one of her many mouse characters (below) show how well she could paint the animal characters she created.

▲ A piece of pottery from ancient Persia (now Iran) dating back to about 1000 B.C. It is brightly decorated with enamel paint.

► A wine pot made of porcelain, made in China during the Sung Dynasty (A.D. 960–1279). The pot sits in a warming bowl shaped like a lotus flower.

▼ A Chinese Ming-period (1368–1644) blue-and-white porcelain vase. Even this long ago, Chinese potters were able to make pots of eggshell thinness.

ors, which add a touch of decoration to the clay. However, earthenware will crack if used over a fire for cooking.

Stoneware is a type of ceramic made with a mixture of clay and crushed rock. When stoneware is fired under very intense heat, the crushed rock melts, filling the pores in the clay. For this reason, stoneware will not leak and does not have to be glazed in order to hold liquids. Stoneware can be used for baking.

The ceramic called *porcelain* was first invented by the Chinese during the Tang Dynasty (A.D. 618–906). Porcelain is made of a white clay mixed with powdered rock. This is fired at temperatures hot enough to melt iron— about 1,560°F (850°C). Porcelain is *translucent* (light can be seen through it) and extremely hard. When porcelain first came to Europe from China in the 1400s, it was called "China ware." The name became popular, and now the term "china" is used for all fine dishes and porcelain objects.

In the 1500s, craftworkers working for the Medici family in Florence, Italy, tried to imitate the Chinese porcelain. They mixed ground-up glass with clay, thinking that glass was what made the Chinese porcelain translucent. In firing, the melted glass caused bubbles and cracks to form. The pottery often lost its shape or became thick and heavy, depending on the amount of glass used. Eventually the Italian potters succeeded in making porcelain with glass, but it was not hard like the Chinese type. Porcelain made with ground glass is called soft porcelain, or Medici porcelain. Chinese porcelain, made with powdered rock, is called hard porcelain.

The Making of Ceramics

Ceramics were made by all ancient peoples. The earliest known ceramics are about 10,000 years old and come from the Middle East. Before pottery was invented, grain was kept in baskets and liquids were kept in bags made of animal skins. Baskets were smeared with clay on the inside to keep grains from dropping through the holes in the weaving. When the basket wore out, the lining of dried clay was left. This was the first pottery.

Since these clay pots were only dried and not fired, liquids made them lose their shape. No one knows how or when firing was invented, but ancient people discovered that if a clay pot was baked in a fire, liquids could no longer harm it. People made pots by lining baskets with soft clay and putting them on a fire. When the baskets burned away, people had fired clay pots with basket-weave designs on their surfaces.

This method of shaping pots took a long time because a new basket had to be woven for every pot. A quicker method was to form the moist clay into long rolls and wind them around and around into the shape of a jar or bowl. The outside surface was then scraped smooth, a design was cut into it, and the pot was then fired.

About 3000 B.C., the *potter's wheel* was invented. A ball of moist clay was placed on the center of the wheel. As the wheel spun around, the potter shaped the clay with his or her fingers. Early potters needed an assistant to turn the wheel. Later, a kick wheel was added so that the potter could use his or her foot to turn the wheel. Modern potter's wheels are electrically operated. Making pottery on a wheel is called "throwing a pot." Wheel-made pottery is always curved or round. Other shapes are formed with the hands or with molds.

Different kinds of clay turn different colors when fired—red, yellow, deep brown, black, off-white, or tan. Potters often dip a pot into *slip,* or liquid clay of another color. After the pot is fired, the potter can scratch through the thin layer of slip to expose the original color of the pot and create a two-color design.

The earliest glazed pottery has been found in the Middle East. The ancient Egyptians used many colors of glaze, especially a deep, bright blue. The Persians worked with special paints, called enamels, that could be used on glaze. Enamels were made of ground glass and produced brilliant colors. People living in the Mesopotamian region developed tin-enamel glaze. A tin mixture was added to clear glaze, producing a milky white color. This white glaze provided a good background to paint on. Tin-enamel glazing became very popular and has been used by people around the world.

The ancient Greeks developed a way of decorating pottery with slip instead of glaze. Greek potters usually used red clay to shape their pottery. Then they used black slip to paint figures and designs on the surface. These are called black-figure vases. Red-figure vases were made by painting the background with black slip and leaving the figures and designs in red. After the slip was painted on and fired, the pottery was polished. Greek craftworkers developed very complicated and delicate designs, often portraying the deeds of their gods and goddesses.

Chinese potters made earthenware, stoneware, and all kinds of glazes and enamels. They also used a process called *underglazing*, painting with colored glazes on the surface of a pot before adding a second coating of glaze. The Chinese often carved their pottery to form raised and lowered areas on the surface.

Until the 1700s, the Chinese were the only people who knew how to make hard porcelain. In 1708, Johann Friedrich Böttger in Dresden, Germany, succeeded in making the first European porcelain.

Ceramics of many kinds have been made in Europe. Beginning in the 1400s, Italian potters made an earthenware with tin-enamel glaze called *majolica*. Majolica ware was colorfully decorated with copies of famous paintings as well as scenes from history and mythology. In France and Germany, tin-enamel ware was called *faïence* because it was first brought to those countries from potteries in Faenza, Italy. Dutch tin-enamel ware is called *delftware* because most of it was made in the town of Delft. Delftware potters copied Chinese designs.

◀ **Greek pots are prized for their beauty, and are often decorated with scenes from the Greek myths. This kind of pot, made between 600 and 530 B.C., is decorated with black figures.**

▼ **European potters attempted to copy Chinese porcelain. This figure was made in 1765 by the Meissen factory near Dresden, Germany.**

◀ **Bone china is made from a mixture of China clay, China stone, and crushed bones. This is mixed with water to make clay. The clay is then made into an object. The object is fired, painted with a glaze, and then fired again.**

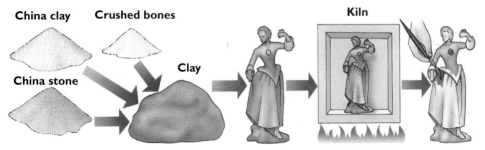

China clay   Crushed bones

China stone

Clay

Kiln

▶ **An elaborate porcelain vase from the Sèvres factory in France, made in about 1785. Sèvres porcelain is richly colored and gilded.**

Perhaps the best-known European maker of stoneware was Josiah Wedgwood of England. He first developed a cream-colored earthenware with transparent glaze that was very strong. It looked like porcelain but was much cheaper and therefore very popular. Wedgwood copied the shapes of ancient Greek pottery in colored stoneware of blue, green, pink, white, and black. He decorated his pottery with a white stone called *jasper,* and this Wedgwood style has since been widely imitated. Wedgwood was also the first person to mass-produce pottery.

Most pottery today is mass-produced in factories. It can be shaped, fired, and decorated quickly and cheaply on an assembly line. Mass-produced decorations are usually applied with *transfers*—printed papers whose designs are fixed to the piece by firing.

LEARN BY DOING

If you would like to try making pottery, you can begin by molding bowls and other simple objects by hand. You can buy modeling clay that will be easy to work and will harden on its own, without having to be fired in a kiln. Then you can go on to more advanced pottery, by joining a class. Your school, community center, or a local art museum may have a kiln and potter's wheel you can use—or they can tell you where the equipment is available.

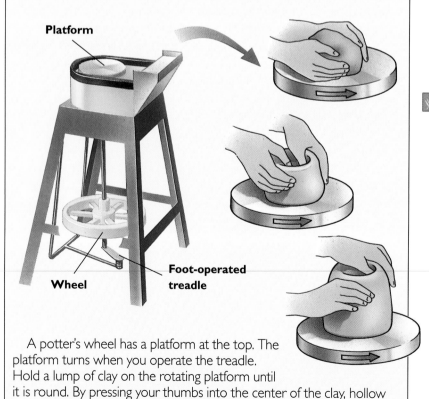

Platform

Wheel

Foot-operated treadle

A potter's wheel has a platform at the top. The platform turns when you operate the treadle. Hold a lump of clay on the rotating platform until it is round. By pressing your thumbs into the center of the clay, hollow out the inside. Finally, by easing your hands upwards, form a tall shape.

POULTRY

Birds raised for their meat and eggs are called poultry. Chickens, ducks, turkeys, geese, guinea fowl (or guinea hen), pheasants, and pigeons can all be poultry birds.

In the United States, about 95 percent of all poultry are chickens. A large industry produces chickens and eggs for market. Only a few chicken farms go through all the steps of raising chickens from eggs, selling the eggs laid by these chickens, and also selling chickens for meat. Most large chicken farms specialize in one of the steps that produce eggs and chickens.

All chickens are descended from a type of pheasant still living in the jungles of India. Careful breeding has produced two different kinds of chicken: chickens that are good for meat and chickens that are good for eggs. Meat chickens should grow fat quickly on a small amount of food. The white Plymouth Rock is the most popular meat chicken. Egg-laying chickens should lay a lot of eggs quickly and not eat or sit very much. White leghorns are the best egg-laying chickens.

Breeders either hatch their own eggs or send them to commercial hatcheries. The eggs are hatched in an *incubator.* An incubator is a heated cabinet that supplies the warmth a mother hen usually supplies for hatching eggs. A large incubator can hold 100,000 eggs. The chicks hatch in about 21 days.

Chicks bred for their meat are called *broiler* chicks. They are bought by broiler growers and put in growing houses with dirt or concrete floors. The chicks are *brooded,* or kept warm, for the first four to six weeks. Then the heat is turned down. They are fed a rich mash of corn, meat, fish, vitamins, and minerals. In eight to nine weeks, they weigh 3 to 4 pounds (1.4 to 1.8 kg). They are then sold as *broilers* or *fryers.* Older, heavier, tougher chickens are sold as *roasters, stewing chickens,* or just plain *fowl.* An unsexed male chicken is called a *capon.*

The female egg-laying chicks, called *pullets,* are sold to egg farmers. The male chicks of egg-laying breeds are usually killed. The pullets are brooded and grown for five months, and then they are put to work laying eggs. On a small farm, a hen might lay eight to ten eggs in a nest and spend three weeks hatching them. But on a large modern egg farm, the eggs are taken away as soon as they are laid, and the hen just keeps laying more eggs. On such a farm, a good white leghorn pullet can lay 250 to 300 eggs a year. After 12 to 15 months, pullets are usually killed and sold as stewing chickens, and the egg farmer buys a new flock of pullets.

▲ **Most poultry comes from large farms, which may have more than 100,000 chickens. Each poultry house contains thousands of birds, which are fed and watered by automatic equipment.**

▼ **Hens begin to lay eggs when they are about 22 weeks old. They lay an egg a day until the nest is full. The hen will then sit on the nest for about three weeks until the young chicks begin to hatch.**

▲ **A cock turkey struts and fans out its feathers in an impressive display.**

> We think of chickens as birds that don't fly. This is not really so. It is possible for a chicken to fly for more than 200 feet (60 m).

▼ **Power is the rate at which "work" is done. One form of energy is converted into another. When a man pushes a heavy truck, chemical energy, used up in his muscles, is converted into heat and into mechanical energy to move the truck.**

Four of every 100 poultry fowl are turkeys. Most American families think of eating turkeys at Thanksgiving and at Christmas, but turkeys can be bought at markets throughout the year. The markets are supplied by a turkey-raising industry. Until about 30 years ago, the average turkey weighed between 16 and 24 pounds (7.3 and 11 kg). Now farmers and scientists have succeeded in breeding smaller turkeys, too. The males weigh about 15 pounds (7 kg) and the females about 8 pounds (3.5 kg). This size turkey is popular with small families for Sunday dinner. There is no turkey egg industry.

Not quite 2 of every 100 poultry fowl are ducks, and almost 1 in 100 is a goose. Ducks and geese are raised for meat and for feathers. The *down* feathers of these two birds are especially soft and are used to stuff pillows and skiers' down jackets. Ducks about eight weeks old are called *ducklings*. They weigh 5 or 6 pounds (2.5 or 3 kg) and are sold for meat. Geese are sold for eating when they are ten weeks old and weigh about 15 pounds (7 kg). Although duck and goose eggs are good to eat, no special industry produces these eggs for market. One kind of duck can lay as many as 360 eggs a year.

In the United States, there are guinea fowl farms in the Midwest and the South. A grown guinea fowl weighs 3 to 3½ pounds (1.4 to 1.6 kg). The pearl (or white) and the lavender guinea fowl are raised as poultry. The pearl has white-dotted,

▲ **A handsome male pheasant. Like many male birds, the male pheasant has colorful plumage to attract a mate.**

purplish gray feathers. Guinea fowl are eaten mostly in restaurants.

Pheasants are wild birds, but a few are raised as poultry. Pheasants ready for market weigh about 5 pounds (2.5 kg) each. They, too, are usually sold to restaurants.

When your great-grandparents wanted to eat a chicken, they may have had to pluck it themselves, or they may have bought a live bird and killed it themselves. Then they had the messy job of cleaning it. Today, most chicken and most other poultry is sold cleaned and packaged. And if your parents don't want to buy a whole bird, they can buy the parts instead—wings, breasts, or legs.

▶▶▶▶ **FIND OUT MORE** ◀◀◀◀
Egg; Game Birds; Incubator; Meat

POWER

Your parents have a powerful car, but the parents of a friend of yours may have one that is more powerful. One car can go much faster than the other, and it can *accelerate* (speed up) much more swiftly. But what does the word "powerful" really mean?

To understand the idea of power,

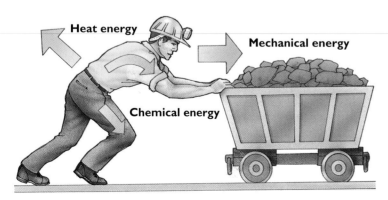

Heat energy

Mechanical energy

Chemical energy

we first have to understand the idea of work. When scientists use the word "work," they do not mean the type of work you have to do at school.

Imagine two machines that can push heavy weights. If one machine pushes a weight twice as heavy as the other does, we say that the machine is doing twice as much work. Likewise, if one machine can push the same weight as the other, but twice as far, we say it is doing twice as much work. To a scientist, the word "work" therefore means the force produced by the machine multiplied by the *distance* over which that force works.

But some machines are able to do a lot more work in a given time than others. If two machines had to push the same weight the same distance, one might be able to do it twice as fast as the other. We say that this machine is twice as *powerful* as the other.

So, when people say that they have a powerful automobile, what they really mean is that the automobile has an engine that can do a lot of work very quickly.

▶▶▶▶ **FIND OUT MORE** ◀◀◀◀
Force

POWHATAN
(about 1550–1618)

Powhatan was a wise and powerful Native American chief. He ruled the Powhatan Confederacy, a group of Algonkian-speaking tribes numbering about 9,000 people. They lived in villages along the coast of Virginia, where the English made their first permanent settlement in America.

Powhatan's real name was Wahunsonacock. But the English colonists called him "Powhatan" after the name of his favorite village. Powhatan was friendly to the settlers and traded with them.

The people in England who had sent the settlers to Virginia wanted to

make a profit on the money they had invested. They demanded that the colonists grow more tobacco. The colonists needed more land, so they began taking Native American land. Naturally, Powhatan and his warriors fought to keep their land.

When Powhatan's daughter, Pocahontas, married a colonist named John Rolfe in 1614, the chief made

▼ According to legend, Powhatan's daughter, Pocahontas, saved the life of Captain John Smith. In this picture, Powhatan looks on as Pocahontas stops the tomahawk of one of his braves.

peace with the English. But he died four years later, and his brother, Opechancanough, attacked the colonists at Jamestown. Finally, in 1644, the Powhatan Confederacy was defeated. The tribes gradually died out.

▶▶▶▶ **FIND OUT MORE** ◀◀◀◀
Algonkian; American History; Native Americans; Jamestown; Pocahontas

PRAIRIE

When pioneers headed West in the 1800s, they took their covered wagons over mountains, across rivers, and through forests. Imagine their surprise when they came to a place where there were no mountains, no rivers, no trees—only tall grass waving in the breeze, as far as they could see! The pioneers had reached the prairies.

Prairie is a French word, meaning "meadow." A prairie is simply a

WHERE TO DISCOVER MORE

Barth, Edna. *Turkeys, Pilgrims, and Indian Corn: The Story of the Thanksgiving Symbols.* New York: Clarion Books, 1975.

Fritz, Jean. *The Double Life of Pocahontas.* New York: Putnam, 1983.

Jones, J.C. *The American Indian in America, in The In America Series.* Minneapolis, MN: Lerner Publs., 1991.

▲ There are many different kinds of grass on the prairies. In some areas it may grow to more than 6 feet (1.8 m) high.

▼ Farmland covers what was once prairie grassland in the midwestern United States. Contour farming, seen here in Nebraska, has crops planted at varying levels along the rolling prairies.

broad, grassy plain found in temperate regions. In Argentina this kind of grassland is called the *pampas*. In Russia, a similar level stretch of land at a higher elevation is called the *steppes*. In South Africa, the high prairie region is called the *veld* or *veldt*. Large stretches of prairie are also found in Hungary, Romania, Brazil, Uruguay, Canada, and the United States. Prairies in the United States spread across Illinois, Iowa, Oklahoma, Texas, Nebraska, Kansas, North and South Dakota, and parts of other states. Alberta, Saskatchewan, and Manitoba are known as the "Prairie Provinces" in Canada.

Little rain falls on the North American prairie regions. Summers are hot and dry. Few trees grow on the land, but the landscape is broken up by scattered, low hills and riverbeds. Prairie grass is coarse and grows from 2 to 6 feet (60 cm to 2 m) high or even taller. There are many different kinds of prairie grass, including big and little bluestem, wild rye, switch grass, June grass, needlegrass, and slough grass. Prairie grass is rooted in thick, rich soil.

Spiders, ants, wasps, beetles, and other insects live among the grasses. Some birds living in the grasslands are hawks, larks, sparrows, prairie chickens, and pheasants. Snakes and toads are common. Prairie dogs, jackrabbits, kangaroo rats, and squirrels live in regions where the grass has been worn down by cattle. Buffalo (bison) once grazed on American prairies, but most of them were killed by hunters.

The pioneers who settled on the big prairies of the Midwest faced many difficulties. They could not break through the dense *sod* (grass-covered surface soil) of the prairies easily with their wooden and iron plows. But in 1837, a blacksmith named John Deere invented the steel plow that cut sharply through the tough soil. With so few trees on the prairies, pioneers (called "sodbusters") made huts out of chunks of sod. Then railroads came to the prairie region, and settlers were able to send crops to market and get lumber and other supplies. Today, grain-growing farms and many cattle ranches are spread across the prairies.

▶▶▶▶ **FIND OUT MORE** ◀◀◀◀
Bison; Grass; Great Plains; Prairie Dog; Westward Movement

PRAIRIE DOG

The prairie dog received its name because it makes a noise similar to a dog's bark. Prairie dogs, also called ground squirrels, are related to both squirrels and marmots.

The prairie dog measures about 14 inches (35 cm) in length, including a bushy tall about 3 inches (8 cm) long. The animal is reddish brown with patches of gray and white. The female prairie dog usually produces four young in a litter. Prairie dogs feed on the vegetation available on dry prairie land.

The prairie dog lives in large underground burrows in the western

United States. These burrows, about 10 feet (3 m) under the ground, have so many tunnels that people call the burrows "towns." Hundreds of prairie dog families live in these towns. A rim of earth around the entrance to the burrow prevents it from flooding. A prairie dog usually stands guard at each entrance to the town. If it sees an enemy, it makes a loud barking noise and everyone runs for home.

Before farmers and cattle ranchers came west, the number of prairie dogs was kept down by their natural enemies, such as weasels, wolves, snakes, and hawks. But when the settlers came, they chased away or killed most of these enemies. As a result, the number of prairie dogs grew larger and larger. In some parts of Texas, the towns extended for hundreds of miles underground. This land could not be used because of the tunnels, so farmers killed many of the prairie dogs. The few towns that remain are mostly in parts where wildlife is protected.

▶ ▶ ▶ ▶ **FIND OUT MORE** ◀ ◀ ◀ ◀
Mammal; Rodent; Squirrel

PRAYER

A prayer is a way of communicating with God. Prayer is practiced differently by people of different religious faiths. It is a form of devotion through which a person can give thanks, ask for help, confess sins, or otherwise approach God. Prayers are often said with the head bowed.

Many Roman Catholics pray with the help of a *rosary,* a circle of 50 beads. From them hangs a *crucifix* (cross) and five more beads—three together and one single bead on either side. The beads are used to count prayers; the Hail Mary is recited on most beads; different prayers are recited on other beads.

▶ ▶ ▶ ▶ **FIND OUT MORE** ◀ ◀ ◀ ◀
Religion
See also names of individual religions

PRECIPITATION

SEE WATER, WATER CYCLE

▲ Prairie dogs live in large communities called towns, each of which is divided into smaller units called *coteries.*

▲ A rosary is used by Roman Catholics to help with concentration while praying. Prayer beads are also used by Buddhists, Hindus, and Muslims.

▲ **Trilobites were crablike animals that lived in the sea more than 340 million years ago.**

▼ **Fossils help scientists reconstruct extinct creatures, such as this pterosaur.**

▼ **The earliest mammals were small and lived in the shadow of the dinosaurs.**

▼ **The first human tools were made from stone. By rubbing two stones together, it was possible to make a sharp edge on one.**

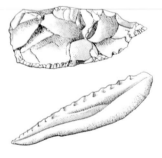

PREDATOR

SEE CARNIVORE, FOOD WEB

PREGNANCY

SEE REPRODUCTION

PREHISTORY

About 5,000 years ago, someone invented writing, and so history began. People could write about the things that happened, and centuries later other people could read what had been written. But human beings existed for several million years before writing was invented, and the Earth was formed several billion years before that. *Prehistory* is the word we use to describe the time before writing was invented.

The study of prehistory is carried out by scientists of several different types. *Cosmologists* are interested in events so far in the past that they happened even before the Earth existed. They try to work out what happened when the universe sprang into existence. *Historical geologists* study rocks to find out what our planet was like millions of years ago. *Paleontologists* study fossils to see what animals and plants were like during prehistory. And *archeologists* look at the remains of prehistoric human beings—their paintings, their bones, and even their garbage heaps—to find out what our distant ancestors were like.

▶▶▶▶ **FIND OUT MORE** ◀◀◀◀
Ancient Civilizations; Archaeology; Dinosaur; Earth History; Fossil; Plants of the Past; Universe

PREPOSITION

SEE PARTS OF SPEECH

PRESIDENCY

The President of the United States, often called the Chief Executive, is the head of the federal government. The President is elected for a four-year term and can serve no more than two terms. A candidate for the Presidency must be a native-born citizen who is at least 35 years old, and has lived in the United States for 14 years before running for office.

Article Two of the U.S. Constitution defines many of the President's powers. The Constitution separates governmental powers into three areas: legislative, executive, and judicial. The executive branch, headed by the President, has the job of enforcing laws made by the legislative branch—Congress. The Constitution also gives the President the duties of commanding the armed forces, making treaties with foreign nations, and appointing government officials. The President can also *pardon* (release from prison) people who have been convicted of crimes—except for government officials who have been impeached—and can also grant *reprieves,* or postponements of punishment. The President plans programs and policies with the executive department heads—the Cabinet—and makes a yearly report to Congress on the state of the union. The President can *veto* (overrule) legislation passed by Congress.

The Presidency has assumed more power through the years, as the problems of daily government of the country have increased. Executive orders issued by the President have the force of law. The President has a great deal of influence on the country's economy through powers given by Congress. The President regulates money loaned by banks and interest charged on loans through the Federal Reserve System, and also regulates interstate *commerce* (buying and selling) through the Interstate Commerce Commission. The President

THE PRESIDENTS OF THE UNITED STATES AND THEIR VICE PRESIDENTS

President	Party	Served	Vice President	Served
1. **George Washington** (1732–1799)	Federalist	1789–1797	John Adams	1789–1797
2. **John Adams** (1735–1826)	Federalist	1797–1801	Thomas Jefferson	1797–1801
3. **Thomas Jefferson** (1743–1826)	Democratic-Republican	1801–1809	Aaron Burr	1801–1805
			George Clinton	1805–1809
4. **James Madison** (1751–1836)	Democratic-Republican	1809–1817	George Clinton	1809–1812
			Elbridge Gerry	1813–1814
5. **James Monroe** (1758–1831)	Democratic-Republican	1817–1825	Daniel D. Tompkins	1817–1825
6. **John Quincy Adams** (1767–1848)	Democratic-Republican	1825–1829	John C. Calhoun	1825–1829
7. **Andrew Jackson** (1767–1845)	Democrat	1829–1837	John C. Calhoun	1829–1832
			Martin Van Buren	1833–1837
8. **Martin Van Buren** (1782–1862)	Democrat	1837–1841	Richard M. Johnson	1837–1841
9. **William H. Harrison** (1773–1841)	Whig	1841	John Tyler	1841
10. **John Tyler** (1790–1862)	Whig	1841–1845		
11. **James K. Polk** (1795–1849)	Democrat	1845–1849	George M. Dallas	1845–1849
12. **Zachary Taylor** (1784–1850)	Whig	1849–1850	Millard Fillmore	1849–1850
13. **Millard Fillmore** (1800–1874)	Whig	1850–1853		
14. **Franklin Pierce** (1804–1869)	Democrat	1853–1857	William R. King	1853
15. **James Buchanan** (1791–1868)	Democrat	1857–1861	John C. Breckinridge	1857–1861
16. **Abraham Lincoln** (1809–1865)	Republican	1861–1865	Hannibal Hamlin	1861–1865
			Andrew Johnson	1865
17. **Andrew Johnson** (1808–1875)	National Union	1865–1869		
18. **Ulysses S. Grant** (1822–1885)	Republican	1869–1877	Schuyler Colfax	1869–1873
			Henry Wilson	1873–1875
19. **Rutherford B. Hayes** (1822–1893)	Republican	1877–1881	William A. Wheeler	1877–1881
20. **James A. Garfield** (1831–1881)	Republican	1881	Chester A. Arthur	1881
21. **Chester A. Arthur** (1830–1886)	Republican	1881–1885		
22. **Grover Cleveland** (1837–1908)	Democrat	1885–1889	Thomas A. Hendricks	1885
23. **Benjamin Harrison** (1833–1901)	Republican	1889–1893	Levi P. Morton	1889–1893
24. **Grover Cleveland** (1837–1908)	Democrat	1893–1897	Adlai E. Stevenson	1893–1897
25. **William McKinley** (1843–1901)	Republican	1897–1901	Garret A. Hobart	1897–1899
			Theodore Roosevelt	1901
26. **Theodore Roosevelt** (1858–1919)	Republican	1901–1909	Charles W. Fairbanks	1905–1909
27. **William H. Taft** (1857–1930)	Republican	1909–1913	James S. Sherman	1909–1912
28. **Woodrow Wilson** (1856–1924)	Democrat	1913–1921	Thomas R. Marshall	1913–1921
29. **Warren G. Harding** (1865–1923)	Republican	1921–1923	Calvin Coolidge	1921–1923
30. **Calvin Coolidge** (1872–1933)	Republican	1923–1929	Charles G. Dawes	1925–1929
31. **Herbert C. Hoover** (1874–1964)	Republican	1929–1933	Charles Curtis	1929–1933
32. **Franklin D. Roosevelt** (1882–1945)	Democrat	1933–1945	John N. Garner	1933–1941
			Henry A. Wallace	1941–1945
			Harry S. Truman	1945
33. **Harry S. Truman** (1884–1972)	Democrat	1945–1953	Alben W. Barkley	1949–1953
34. **Dwight D. Eisenhower** (1890–1969)	Republican	1953–1961	Richard M. Nixon	1953–1961
35. **John F. Kennedy** (1917–1963)	Democrat	1961–1963	Lyndon B. Johnson	1961–1963
36. **Lyndon B. Johnson** (1908–1973)	Democrat	1963–1969	Hubert H. Humphrey	1965–1969
37. **Richard M. Nixon** (1913–1994)	Republican	1969–1974	Spiro T. Agnew	1969–1973
			Gerald R. Ford	1973–1974
38. **Gerald R. Ford** (1913–	Republican	1974–1977	Nelson A. Rockefeller	1974–1977
39. **James E. Carter** (1924–	Democrat	1977–1981	Walter F. Mondale	1977–1981
40. **Ronald W. Reagan** (1911–	Republican	1981–1989	George Bush	1981–1989
41. **George H. Bush** (1924–	Republican	1989–1993	James Danforth Quayle	1989–1993
42. **William J. Clinton** (1946–	Democrat	1993–	Albert Gore	1993–

► **The seal of the President of the United States.**

QUIZ

1. Which branch of the U.S. government is the President in charge of?
2. How many executive departments are under the President's direction?
3. Who was the youngest President (at the time of his inauguration)?
4. Who was the longest-serving President? And the shortest?
5. How many Vice Presidents went on to become President?

(Answers on page 2176)

▼ **The Oval Office in the White House is where the President carries out his daily duties.**

presents the yearly national budget to Congress. The President is also in charge of U.S. relations with other countries and can make agreements with other countries that are as binding as treaties (which must have the approval of the Senate).

The ability to appoint federal officials and remove them from office also gives the President a great deal of power. Some of the most important appointments are those the President makes to the U.S. Supreme Court. These justices often serve for many years after the President has left office. According to the Constitution, the Senate must approve the President's appointments, but in practice, the Senate considers only high ranking officials. Appointment to governmental office is the most important way in which a President can repay those who have worked in his campaign.

The size of the executive branch can give you a good idea of the power and responsibilities of the Presidency. Under the direction of the President are the 14 executive departments (each employing a large number of people) and many independent

agencies, which are often as large as the departments. The executive branch employs most civil service employees—over two million people. Each President also organizes a group of assistants, called the Executive Office, who work in the White House and other buildings.

The Constitution provides for orderly succession to the Presidency. The Twenty-fifth Amendment, adopted in 1967, states that if a President dies or resigns before the term of office ends, the Vice President becomes President. If this should occur, the new President appoints a new Vice President, with the approval of Congress.

► ► ► ► **FIND OUT MORE** ◄ ◄ ◄ ◄
Cabinet, United States; Congress, United States; Impeachment; Legislature; United States Government; Vice President

PRESLEY, ELVIS (1935–1977)

Who was the first "king" of rock 'n' roll? Most people would answer: Elvis Presley. Elvis Aaron Presley was a star of pop music. His name and songs were known all over the world from the moment he burst onto the scene in 1956.

Elvis Presley was born in Tupelo, Mississippi, on January 8, 1935. He made his first record while working as a truck driver singing country-and-western music. He was also influenced by black rhythm-and-blues singers, and brought black music to the attention of many people who had never listened to it before.

In 1956, Presley had his first hit record: "Heartbreak Hotel." He went on to an amazing career as an entertainer, making hit records that sold millions of copies and becoming an international idol to millions of fans. He also made a number of films, such as *Love Me Tender* and *Jailhouse Rock*.

Presley was admired and imitated by numerous other pop performers. Fans all over the world mourned his death in 1977. He died at the age of 42 in Memphis, Tennessee, where his career had begun. However, Elvis Presley is just about as popular today as he was when he was performing.

PRESSURE

Imagine blowing up a balloon. As you blow more air into the balloon, it gets bigger and bigger. If you blow in too much air, the balloon bursts. The pressure of the air becomes too great, and the rubber breaks.

What is pressure? Scientists say that it is force per unit area acting on a surface. This is hard to understand. But imagine you have blown up the balloon and now touch it with a pin.

Excited gas molecules under pressure

You don't have to push the pin very hard to burst the balloon. But you would have to use quite a lot of force to burst the balloon by squeezing it between your hands. This is because your hands have a far greater area than the point of the pin. The larger the area of the object you press against the balloon, the more force you need to use to burst it.

But why does a balloon get bigger as you blow more air into it? You are

making the pressure of the air inside the balloon greater than the pressure of the air outside it. There are many more air molecules inside the balloon than there would be in a similar volume of "normal" air. The molecules are moving around very rapidly, and lots of them hit the inside of the balloon every second— far more than are hitting it from the outside every second.

If you heat the air molecules inside the balloon, they travel even faster, and so the balloon gets bigger. Put a balloon in a hot bath, and see how it has changed when you pull it out of the hot water. But it will soon go back to its old size as the air inside it cools.

▶▶▶▶ **FIND OUT MORE** ◀◀◀◀
Atmosphere; Force

PRIESTLEY, JOSEPH (1733–1804)

Joseph Priestley was a British clergyman who is remembered for his chemical experiments. Both he and a Swedish scientist, Karl Wilhelm Scheele, are credited with the discovery of oxygen.

Priestley was born at Fieldhead, England. He studied for the Presbyterian ministry and then served as minister in several churches. Priestley was interested in science. He once heard Benjamin Franklin lecture in London on electricity, and he became very interested in the subject. With Franklin's encouragement, Priestley published *The History and Present State of Electricity* in 1767. Priestley is credited with the discovery of *hydrochloric acid, nitrous oxide* (laughing gas), and *sulfur dioxide*. He made his most important discovery in 1774. He heated the compound *mercuric oxide* and obtained a gas. This gas later became known as oxygen.

Priestley continued his work as a minister, becoming a Unitarian. He wrote a number of books on social

▲ Elvis Presley, the "king" of rock 'n' roll.

◀ **Pressure is exerted by a gas, because its molecules bounce off the sides of the container. If the gas is compressed, the pressure is higher, because there is less space (*volume*) for the same molecules to move around in, so there is more force per unit area.**

▲ **Joseph Priestley, English scientist.**

Joseph Priestley accidentally discovered that carbon dioxide dissolved in water has a pleasant, tart taste. Today, this solution is called soda water.

and religious subjects. Because of his sympathy with the French Revolution, a mob in Birmingham, England, burned Priestley's house and destroyed his books and scientific instruments. Priestley left England and went to the United States in 1791. He lived the rest of his life in Northumberland, Pennsylvania.

▶▶▶▶ **FIND OUT MORE** ◀◀◀◀
Chemistry; Element; Franklin, Benjamin; Oxygen

PRIMATE

SEE APE; HUMAN BEING

PRIME MINISTER

Many nations are governed by a legislative assembly or parliament. These assemblies often include a group of particularly important government officials, called ministers. The chief minister is often known as the prime ("first") minister or premier. He or she runs the government and sometimes has more power than the head of state.

The name "prime minister" was first used in Great Britain in the 1700s. King George I, who came to the throne in 1714, left most of the business of government to Parliament. Sir Robert Walpole, the strongest minister in Parliament, became leader of the government, instead of the king. For many years

since then, the prime minister has been the leader of the *majority* (largest) party in Parliament. One of the greatest British prime ministers was Sir Winston Churchill, who led Britain during World War II.

The British prime minister chooses a special council, or *cabinet*, of ministers. He or she usually follows their advice. Some strong prime ministers, such as William Gladstone in the 1800s, have acted against the wishes of the cabinet. But if more than half the members of Parliament vote against the prime minister, he or she must resign or call a new election, or both.

Most countries that were once part of the British Empire—such as Canada, Australia, and India—have a parliamentary government run by a prime minister. Some other nations, such as Spain, Italy, and France, have similar governments. The chief minister in these three countries is also called the prime minister.

▶▶▶▶ **FIND OUT MORE** ◀◀◀◀
Churchill, Winston; George, Kings of England; Government; Parliament

PRINCE EDWARD ISLAND

Prince Edward Island is the smallest of the ten Canadian provinces and is one of the four Maritime Provinces. It is about twice the size of Rhode Island, the smallest U.S. state, but its population is much less. However, despite being small in size, the province is more densely populated than any other Canadian province.

The province, known also as P.E.I., is an island in the Gulf of St. Lawrence. Northumberland Strait separates it from New Brunswick and Nova Scotia. At its closest point, it is 9 miles (14.5 km) from New Brunswick. Cape Breton Island is to the east.

Prince Edward Island is about 120 miles (195 km) long, with dozens of

▲ Lester B. Pearson was Canadian prime minister from 1963 to 1968.

▶ Indira Gandhi, prime minister of India, who was assassinated by her own Sikh bodyguards on October 31, 1984.

PRINCE EDWARD ISLAND

Capital and largest city
Charlottetown
(17,000 people)

Area
2,180 square miles
(5,646 sq. km)

Population
139,400 people

Entry into Confederation
July 1, 1873

Principal river
East River (tidal inlet)

Highest point
Bonshaw Hills
465 feet (142 m)

Famous people
Lucy Maud Montgomery

▲ An attractive weatherboard lighthouse keeps a vigil for passing ships along Wood Island, one of the many small islets around Prince Edward Island.

▲ Conifer trees stand tight by the coastline along Murray Head, on Prince Edward Island.

North Cape

Tignish

Alberton

O'Leary

West Point

Cascumpec Bay

Egmont Bay

GULF OF ST. LAWRENCE

Malpeque Bay

New London Bay

St. Eleanors
Miscouche
Summerside

Kensington

North Rustico

Grand Tracadie

Morell

St. Peters

East Point

Souris

Bedeque Bay

Winsloe

Sherwood

Borden

Charlottetown
Bunbury
Cornwall
Southport

Montague R.

Georgetown
Cardigan Bay

Montague

Hillsborough Bay

Murray River

Murray Harbour

Northumberland Strait

0   20   40 Miles
0   20   40   60 Kilometers
© 1994 GeoSystems, an R.R. Donnelley & Sons Company

▲ The lady's slipper orchid is the provincial flower of Prince Edward Island.

▲ This farmhouse, believed to have been used as a setting for the book *Anne of Green Gables* by Lucy Maud Montgomery, is in Prince Edward Island National Park. It is open to the public.

The Confederation Chamber in the Provincial Building in Charlottetown, Prince Edward Island, remains furnished as it was in 1864 when the Fathers of Confederation met there to plan the union of Canada. The building is often called the "birthplace of Canada."

sandy beaches. It ranges from about 2 to 35 miles (3 to 55 km) in width. The soil is rich and dark red in color and is ideal for farming. Its climate is kept mild by the ocean surrounding it, and the summer nearly always has fine weather. The beaches of Prince Edward Island have some of the warmest water north of Virginia!

About one-third of the island's population is of Scottish descent, one-third is English, one-fifth Irish, and one-sixth French. There are only about 300 people who are descendants of the original Micmac population.

The province is known for its potatoes and dairy products. Vegetables and flowers grow so well here that the island is known as the "Garden of the Gulf." While farming is the most important occupation on the island, manufacturing and fisheries employ many people. Lobsters and oysters harvested here reach markets in Canada and New England. Silver fox and mink are raised for their fur.

The province is a fine vacation place. Camping, fishing, and swimming are enjoyed at Prince Edward Island National Park and in other areas. Deep-sea fishing is excellent, and horse racing, golf, and other holiday activities are popular.

The children's novel *Anne of Green Gables* tells of life in Prince Edward Island in the late 1800s. Thousands of visitors come to the island each year to see the countryside that was so vividly described in the book.

Jacques Cartier, a French explorer, discovered the island on his first voyage in 1534. The French were the first to colonize it, but it later became British and, in 1873, joined the new nation of Canada.

In 1992, provincial leaders were discussing plans to build a causeway to link P.E.I. with the New Brunswick mainland.

▶▶▶▶ **FIND OUT MORE** ◀◀◀◀
Canada; New Brunswick; Nova Scotia

☼ PRINTING

When writing or pictures are reproduced on sheets of paper by contact with an inked surface, we say that the sheets are printed. Printing is one of the world's greatest inventions, for it allows thousands, even millions, of people to receive information or enjoy works of art. Stories, music, news, business information—all are printed, and modern society needs each of them.

Printing was first invented by the Chinese about A.D. 868. Chinese *characters* (symbols that stand for words) were carved onto blocks so that they were raised from the surface. When ink was applied to the raised characters and paper pressed against them, the ink from the raised characters was transferred to the paper. These carved blocks were the first kind of type. Sometime during the A.D. 1000s, the Chinese also invented movable type. Each character was carved on a separate block, so that they could be used over and over in any combination that was needed.

Modern printing began in Europe in the 1450s, when Johannes Gutenberg cast metal *type,* one piece for each letter, in molds. Many letters, exactly alike, could easily be cast for the printer to make into sentences. The old handwritten book was soon replaced, for printing was much faster. A sheet of paper was laid on the type, the press was screwed down, and thousands of letters appeared on the paper at once. Printing was a great help in the "revival of learning" in the Renaissance. Printing presses were quickly established all over Europe and eventually in the American colonies and elsewhere. During the 1800s and 1900s, a great many inventions improved the speed and accuracy of the printing process.

The Germans began to operate printing presses by steam power instead of by hand in about 1811. About 35 years later in America, the type was put into a cylinder, not into a flatbed. The cylinder could revolve and make more impressions in less time than it took to press paper to a flat bed of type. Still later, another American put revolving cylinders of type together with rotating rolls of paper. In 1884 a machine was invented that could set type. This meant that letters to make words no longer had to be set by hand.

Basic Kinds of Printing

There are three basic kinds of printing *letterpress*, *gravure* (or *intaglio*), and *lithography*.

Letterpress printing is done with type in which the printing surface is raised above the surface of the metal. The letters are inked with a roller and pressed against paper to make the impression. Letterpress is commonly used for newspapers.

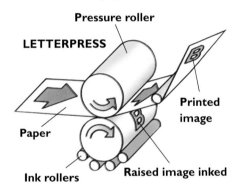

Gravure printing is done with metal plates that have letters or designs set below the surface. These hollowed-out areas are filled with ink, and paper is forced against them with great pressure. This causes the ink to be transferred to the paper.

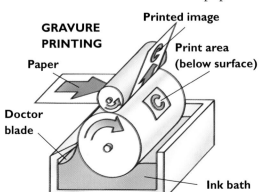

▲ **Johannes Gutenberg inspects a sheet that has just come from his new printing press. Once printing with movable type began, books were produced more quickly and cheaply. Only the rich, however, could afford them or knew how to read.**

Engraving, a gravure process using deep cuts in the metal, can be seen on wedding invitations and other very formal printed materials.

In lithography, the printing surface is neither raised nor sunken. Lithography is based on the principle that grease and water will not mix. If you draw a picture with a crayon, then sprinkle water on it, you will see that the water soaks the paper but makes tight little globs on the wax.

The lettering or other material to be lithographed is put on the printing

◀ **In letterpress printing, the image to be printed exists as a raised area on a lower base.**

◀ **In litho printing, the image is on the surface of the printing plate, and is treated to attract grease-based printing ink and to repel water. In offset litho printing, the ink is *offset* (transferred) to a rubber roller before being applied to the paper.**

◀ **In gravure printing the image is in shallow "holes" below the surface of the plate or roller.**

surface—a metal plate or a special stone—with a greasy substance that attracts a special greasy ink. The surface is wet before printing, so that the ink is easily removed from the areas

▶ To print a color picture by offset lithography, it is first photographed through four color filters. Then a printing plate is made for each color. The yellow plate is printed first, then come the magenta and cyan plates. The black plate is printed last. Mixed together these four colors give the effect of all other colors.

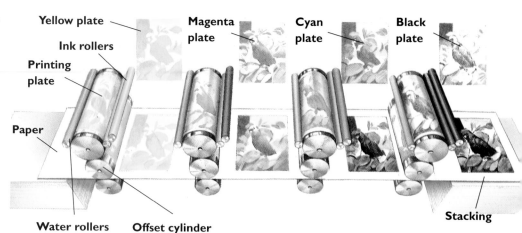

Yellow plate
Ink rollers
Printing plate
Paper
Magenta plate
Cyan plate
Black plate
Water rollers
Offset cylinder
Stacking

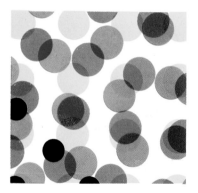

▲ If you look at any picture in this Learning Library through a magnifying glass, you will see that it is made up of lots of colored dots. Tones are created by varying the size of the dots.

▲ "Hot metal" typesetting used the letterpress principle of inking a raised surface. Each letter was made from molten metal as it was typed into a keyboard. This method is now rare.

that are not to print. Then the surface is ready for printing. In *offset lithography*, the ink is *offset* (transferred) to a rubber roller, called a *blanket*, which does the actual printing. This allows the plate to be an inexpensive, thin one, since it is pressing against soft rubber, not against the bed that holds the paper. Photo-offset developed from the use of photography and of the rubber transfer cylinder.

Kinds of Presses

The machine that brings paper into contact with an inked surface to make an *impression* is called a *press*. There are three basic types of presses: the *platen*, the *cylinder*, and the *rotary* press.

The platen press has a heavy, flat piece of metal that presses the paper against the inked surface to make an impression. The cylinder press makes an impression by pressing the paper against the inked surface with a large roller, called a cylinder. The rotary press uses a very large cylinder onto which several lithographic plates can be attached. As the cylinder revolves, it presses the inked type against the paper and makes an impression.

Cylinder and rotary presses can sometimes print on both sides of the paper at once, in which case they are called *cylinder-perfector* or *rotary-perfector* presses. Some presses are called *sheet-fed*. This means that paper is put into the press in the form

of large sheets. Web presses are those that take paper in the form of long continuous rolls (called "webs"). As the printed paper comes out of the machine, the web press cuts and folds it.

Photoengraving

The process of putting pictures into print is called *photoengraving*. Pictures are usually printed in black and white, in two-color (black plus a second color), or in four-color. Four-color printing is the combining of the colors red, yellow, blue, and black to make all other possible colors. The three types of photoengraving are *line*, *halftone*, and *color*. Each is used for certain kinds of pictures.

Line engraving is used to print pictures, such as cartoons, that are composed of lines and have no shading. A photograph is made of the drawing, and the negative is placed on a sheet of light-sensitive metal. When light hits the metal, the surface not covered by the dark parts of the negative goes through a chemical change that makes the surface able to pick up ink. When printed, a copy of the original drawing results.

Halftone engraving is more complicated. It is the method used for printing pictures that do have shading. If you look closely at a newspaper photograph, you will see that the picture is printed with tiny dots. Dark areas of the picture have a heavier concentration of black dots

---

---

than do the light areas. Shades of gray result from a greater or lesser number of dots. These dots are made by placing a screen of tiny crisscrossed lines over the original picture. When the picture is photographed through the screen, it comes out on the negative as a mass of tiny dots. The dots are transferred to a light-sensitive metal plate, which is inked and printed.

The color engraving process is similar to that of halftone, except that four separate negatives must be made, one for each basic color—red, yellow, blue, and black. When the metal plates are made (one for each color), the dots show up in a different pattern for each plate. On the press, the four plates are inked, each with a separate color. As paper is fed through the press, the color plates print consecutively, on exactly the same place on the paper. The four colors combine and the result is a copy of the original.

▶▶▶▶ **FIND OUT MORE** ◀◀◀◀
Book; Communication; Graphic Arts; Gutenberg, Johannes; Ink; Magazine; Newspaper; Publishing; Renaissance; Typesetting

PRISM

SEE COLOR

PRISON

If a person is convicted of a crime, he or she may be locked up in a *prison*, a special enclosed building that is patrolled by armed guards. A prisoner is separated from the rest of the community and loses the freedom to mix freely with society.

Until the Middle Ages, prisons were reserved for people who had committed major crimes, such as murder. In the 1500s, the courts began to sentence people to prison for

LEARN BY DOING

You can print letters or designs by cutting them into the surface of a sliced potato. Dip your block into paint or ink and press it onto a sheet of paper. You will need to cut away all the parts that you do not want to print. Letters have to be cut back to front to print the right way.

committing lesser crimes, such as theft. People were even sent to prison for owing bills they could not pay. Men and women of all ages were herded together in filthy, crowded prisons. They were treated brutally, fed very badly, and were often forced to do hard work. Beginning in the late 1700s, some people began to work to improve conditions in prisons. They believed that they could reform criminals. Their beliefs developed into *penology*, the study of prison management and criminal reform.

Although efforts are still being made to improve prisons, many prisoners today still live under crowded conditions, have little to eat, and are sometimes mistreated by other prisoners. A prisoner's activities may be

▼ Young inmates, most of them boys, exercise in a prison yard in London, England, in the early 1800s. Prisons at that time were often dirty and overcrowded.

▲ **The storming of the Bastille, a fortress-prison in Paris, on July 14, 1789, marked the start of the French Revolution.**

> The longest recorded prison sentence in U.S. history was served by Paul Geidel, convicted of second degree murder. When he was released in 1980, he had spent 68 years, eight months, and two days in prison.

restricted to sleeping in a cell on a small cot, going to the dining hall to eat or outside to a recreation area, and back again to the cell, always under the watchful eye of a guard.

Many prisons today are set up like small cities with laundries, dry cleaners, printing plants, laboratories, and other work areas where prisoners can work and learn a trade or skill. Prisoners may receive some pay for their work. They may work around the prison doing carpentry, masonry, cooking, electrical work, and farming. Some prisoners are clerks, typists, and dental technicians. Many prisons operate their own factories, where automobile license plates, road signs, and other products used by the state or national government are manufactured. Sometimes, a prison may have schools where prisoners can take high school and college courses. *Psychiatrists* (doctors who treat mental illness) and other counselors may help prisoners with their personal problems.

A prisoner with a good behavior record is often given greater freedom and special privileges. One with an excellent record may be made a *trusty* and be allowed to work outside the prison. Trusties may also live in special areas outside the prison. If

prisoners behave well over a long period of time, they may be put on *parole*. This means that they will be released before their prison terms have expired, on the condition that they continue to show good behavior.

Much of their prison experience may be seen as preparation for parole. The prisoners are periodically examined to check on their progress. Eventually each prisoner may be eligible to come up before a parole board. The board determines whether or not the prisoner is sufficiently rehabilitated and not likely to commit another crime. If this is the case, the board may grant parole. The prisoner is then placed under the supervision of a parole officer, who is based in the prisoner's home community. Before this happens, however, the prisoner must have served a specified period of his or her sentence.

Prisons in the United States are operated by three levels of government. Local jails are run by cities and counties. State prisons are maintained by individual states. Federal penitentiaries are operated by the federal government. If a person breaks a city or county law, he or she will go to a city or county jail. Those convicted of violating state and federal laws serve sentences in state or federal prisons. U.S. prisons vary throughout the country. Bad conditions in some prisons have caused prisoners to riot and to fight their guards.

In 1971, one of the worst prison riots in U.S. history occurred at the Attica Correctional Facility in Attica, New York. Mistreatment of prisoners and racial tension were blamed for the riot, in which 32 prisoners and 11 guards were killed. State troopers regained control of the Attica prison after four days. In 1980, another violent uprising occurred at the state penitentiary in Santa Fe, New Mexico. Overcrowding of prisoners was the main cause. This riot left 33 persons dead.

Detention homes are special prisons for people who have committed crimes but are below the legal age at which they can be tried. These prisons are usually *minimum security* prisons. This means that there are fewer guards and fewer restrictions on a prisoner's activities than there would be in most prisons. Detention homes, or reform schools, try to operate like schools and help young people return to the community.

Penologists believe that a prison should not be just a place of punishment, but should also help to *rehabilitate* prisoners. Rehabilitation means that prisoners are helped to become better people, so that when they leave prison they may get jobs and not commit crimes again.

▶▶▶▶ **FIND OUT MORE** ◀◀◀◀
Crime; Juvenile Delinquency; Murder; Trial

PRIVATEERS

SEE PIRATES AND PRIVATEERS

PROGRAM, COMPUTER

SEE COMPUTER

PROHIBITION

The word *prohibit* means to forbid something. The term *prohibition* in U.S. history has usually meant a law forbidding the making and selling of alcoholic drinks. Many American states passed prohibition laws during the 1800s. In 1919, Congress passed the Eighteenth Amendment to the Constitution of the United States. It prohibited the manufacture and sale of all alcoholic drinks. A famous national prohibition law called the *Volstead Act* was passed in that year to enforce and regulate the Eighteenth Amendment. The people who supported the Volstead Act hoped it

would stop people from drinking.

But drinking did not stop—illegal drinking places called "speak-easies" opened. Gangsters made huge amounts of money buying, making, and selling illegal liquor. Some people made their own liquor at home. A great deal of liquor was smuggled in from other countries. Also, the government lost millions of dollars in liquor taxes. In 1933, Congress passed the Twenty-first Amendment, which repealed the Eighteenth Amendment. The making and selling of alcoholic beverages was then no longer against the law.

▶▶▶▶ **FIND OUT MORE** ◀◀◀◀
Alcoholic Beverages

PROKOFIEV, SERGEI (1891–1953)

Have you ever heard the story *of Peter and the Wolf* set to music? This unique musical work was created by the Russian composer, Sergei Prokofiev. The characters in the tale are played by instruments of the orchestra. Peter, a little boy who sets out to catch a wolf, is played by the violins. Peter's grandfather, who tries to keep Peter from catching the wolf, is played by a bassoon. Peter has two companions who help him—a duck (played by an oboe) and a bird (played by a flute). The wolf that Peter catches is played by French horns. And the three hunters who help take the wolf to the zoo are played by trumpets and trombones. During a performance of *Peter and the Wolf,* a narrator tells the story as the orchestra plays the various parts.

Prokofiev was born on a country estate at Sontsovka (now called Krasnoye) in southern Russia. His mother was his first music teacher, and encouraged him to start studying music at a very early age. By the time he was 9 years old, Prokofiev

The most notorious prison settlement was the French Devil's Island, off the coast of French Guiana in South America. It has been estimated that of the 70,000 prisoners deported to Devil's Island, only about 2,000 ever returned.

It is said that Al Capone, the gangster and bootlegger who made and sold liquor during Prohibition in the United States, made $60 million a year from his illegal activities. Al Capone's gang killed seven members of a rival bootlegging gang on St. Valentine's Day, 1929. This became known as the St. Valentine's Day Massacre.

▲ Sergei Prokofiev, Russian composer.

▶ **Prometheus chained to a rock, with an eagle tearing out his liver.**

Listen to how you pronounce "Mary," "marry," and "merry." Many Americans think that these words are *homonyms*, words that sound the same but have different meanings. British people, however, pronounce each of these words differently.

▼ Many words are spelled similarly, but pronounced differently. Shortening or lengthening the vowel sounds makes the difference. "Dessert" has a "long e" while "desert" has a "short e."

Desert

Dessert

had already written a three-act opera entitled *The Giant.*

Prokofiev was admitted to the St. Petersburg Conservatory of Music at age 13. He graduated seven years later with high honors. When he was 23, Prokofiev won the Rubinstein Prize (an award for excellence in musical composition) for his *First Piano Concerto.*

Prokofiev's music is modern in form and sound. His *Classical Symphony* was written as if an earlier composer, such as Mozart, were writing music in the 1900s. *The Love for Three Oranges* was written for the Chicago Opera Company.

Prokofiev left Russia at the outbreak of the revolution in 1917, living in exile in the United States and France. In 1933, he returned with his family to settle in the former Soviet Union. In 1948, Prokofiev and other leading Soviet musicians were accused by Soviet authorities of composing music that was "distorted" and not appropriate for Soviet citizens to listen to. Despite this censure, Prokofiev continued to compose until his death in Moscow in 1953. The Communist Party finally changed its opinion of Prokofiev's music. His *Ninth Symphony* was awarded the Lenin Prize in 1958.

▶▶▶▶ **FIND OUT MORE** ◀◀◀◀
Composer; Music;
Opera; Orchestras and Bands

PROMETHEUS

Prometheus was a hero in Greek myths. He belonged to the Titans, a race of gods.

Prometheus often helped *mortals* (ordinary humans, as opposed to gods). He stole fire from the gods and gave it to the human race. This angered Zeus, the leader of the gods. He had Prometheus chained to a rock. Each day an eagle came and tore out his liver. Every night Zeus

made the liver grow back again. Prometheus could have brought his suffering to an end by telling Zeus a certain secret, but Prometheus courageously refused to do this. Because of this, he was one of the great mythological heroes of mankind. Finally Hercules, a famous Greek hero, killed the eagle and freed Prometheus.

▶▶▶▶ **FIND OUT MORE** ◀◀◀◀
Hercules; Pandora

PRONOUN

SEE PARTS OF SPEECH

PRONUNCIATION

When you speak a language, you are pronouncing sounds, which form meaningful words. The particular way in which you speak it is called *pronunciation.* Perhaps you have noticed that people from different areas of the United States pronounce words differently. In many so-called southern accents and in the Bostonian accent, the "r" sound is replaced by an "ah" sound. "Larger" is pronounced "lahjah," and "garden" is pronounced "gahden." People in some places pronounce "oily" as "early" and "early" as "oily."

English pronunciation also differs in different parts of the world. For example, many British people pronounce "been" as "bean," "secretary" as "secratree," and "better" as "bettah." The Australian English pronunciation of "mate" "race," and "pail" would sound like "might," "rice," and "pile" to someone from the United States.

The pronunciation of languages keeps changing, because the people who speak them keep changing. The word "been," for example, was pronounced "bin" or "ben" by English people in the 1600s. English settlers in the New World also pronounced "been" as "bin" or "ben." But American settlers became cut off from the everyday speech of people in England. Today, the British pronunciation of "been" has changed to "bean," while the American pronunciation has remained "bin" or "ben," just as it was in England in the 1600s.

The English language has no strict set of rules for correct pronunciation. People usually adapt their pronunciation to the way others around them are speaking. In studying a foreign language, you must learn to pronounce words in a new way. If you use American English pronunciation when speaking French, for example, French people will not be able to understand you easily. If a French person speaks English totally with French pronunciation, you will have trouble understanding him or her.

The best way to find out the correct pronunciation of a word is to look it up in a dictionary. Each entry word is respelled in a special way, often using special letters and markings, to show you how it is pronounced. The *pronunciation key* is at the front of the dictionary.

▶▶▶▶ **FIND OUT MORE** ◀◀◀◀
Dictionary; English Language; Languages; Speech

PROPAGANDA

Propaganda is a way of attempting to change public opinion through written or spoken messages. Propaganda presents only one side of an issue. Its purpose is to persuade people to have a favorable opinion of that viewpoint. People are subjected to propaganda every day through television, radio, movies, magazines, newspapers, books, and posters. Propaganda is used by and is aimed at individuals, businesses, religious groups, political organizations, and governments. When propaganda is honestly used, it is a fair method of presenting one viewpoint, with facts to support it, to the public. When propaganda is misused, it twists facts and presents inaccurate information.

Industries and other special interest groups use propaganda through advertising and other kinds of public relations. When a company advertises its products, it tries to make you want to use them. So the company tells you only the good things about its products. For example, the manufacturers of a detergent will tell you only how well the detergent cleans, how good it smells, and how cheap it is. They will *not* tell you that the detergent may pollute the water.

During elections, political parties use propaganda in publicity campaigns to persuade people to vote for their candidates. In wartime, nations use propaganda to convince their own citizens that the war is necessary. Nations also use propaganda to try to persuade the enemy to give up. In peacetime, nations use propaganda to persuade their citizens and the rest of the world that the government's actions are right.

Everyone is exposed to a great deal of propaganda. An individual should form an opinion only after hearing both sides of an issue, not just what one side chooses to make public.

▶▶▶▶ **FIND OUT MORE** ◀◀◀◀
Advertising; Public Relations

The British writer George Bernard Shaw claimed that, according to pronunciation rules of English, "ghoti" could be pronounced "fish." Say *gh* as in "rough," *o* as in "women," and *ti* as in "nation," and you will see what he meant.

在毛澤東的勝利旗幟下前進

▲ One of the most influential forms of propaganda in modern times was the little red book *Quotations from the Works of Mao Tse-tung,* in China. In the late 1960s, all Chinese had to have a copy— making it probably the most printed publication ever (after the Bible).

A large number of animal bones, with the earliest examples of Chinese writing, have been dug up near the city of Anyang. Many of these bones were used in fortune-telling, and are known as "oracle bones." Shoulder blades were the most commonly used bones.

▼ Daniel, the Old Testament prophet, was condemned to the lions' den for praying to his Jewish God. After surviving a night without a scratch from the lions, he was released.

PROPAGATION

SEE PLANT; REPRODUCTION

PROPHET

A *prophet* is a person believed to have powers of knowing the future. Great kings once employed prophets to advise them. Much ancient pagan prophecy was based on the idea of *fate,* which caused everything to happen, or on the idea that gods and spirits control everything that happens in the world. Prophets were considered to be the "keepers of secret wisdom" by which they were able to know of things to come.

All primitive people have had *shamans* (witch doctors or medicine men) who were believed to be able to contact the spirits and know the future. The ancient Greeks had prophetesses called *sibyls* or *oracles* who were located at the temples of various gods and goddesses. Babylonian prophets, called *magi,* predicted the future by gazing into crystal balls or by using *astrology* (reading the stars). The prophets of ancient Rome, called *augurs,* predicted events by "reading" the *entrails* (internal organs) of dead animals.

According to legend, one augur warned Julius Caesar to "beware the Ides [the fifteenth] of March." On that day, Caesar was murdered.

Prophets throughout the world have tried to predict the future by watching for *omens.* Omens were things that happened in nature, such as a dark cloud appearing at a certain place or a particular bird flying in a certain direction. People believed these omens were signs or warnings of future events.

The Hebrew and Islamic prophets differed from the pagan ones in several ways. They believed in a single, all-powerful God rather than in many gods or spirits. Instead of using crystal balls, entrails, or astrology, they regarded themselves as directly inspired by God. And unlike the pagans, they were concerned with the eternal principles of good and evil, not with what certain gods happened to want at the moment.

Feeling as they did, the Hebrew and Islamic prophets preached the word of God, reminding people of His laws and threatening with punishment those who did not obey. They foretold the future when a person or nation was to be punished, but were more concerned with urging people to reform.

Some of the best-known Hebrew prophets were Isaiah, Jeremiah, Ezekiel, Daniel, Jonah, Hosea, and Amos. Their prophecies are contained in the Old Testament of the Bible. Fulfillment of many of those prophecies, Christians believe, can be found in the New Testament. Muhammad was the great prophet of Islam. His writings are contained in the Koran.

▶▶▶▶ **FIND OUT MORE** ◀◀◀◀
Astrology; Bible; Fortune-telling; Gods and Goddesses; Koran; Magic; Religion; Superstition; Witchcraft

PROTECTIVE COLORING

The next time you walk in the woods or fields, look around very carefully. You may be surprised at the number of animals you can spot in the trees and shadows! Many animals have a color or a pattern of colors that matches their surroundings and protects them from enemies. A color pattern that protects an animal is called protective coloration, or protective coloring.

The back of a fawn has broad stripes of two shades of brown. White spots speckle the brown. When a fawn lies down on the floor of the forest, its stripes and spots look almost exactly like the pattern made by sunlight shining through the leaves of trees and bushes. People or

other animals can look at a fawn without realizing they are seeing anything but the sun-speckled ground. This is an example of protective coloring. Animals of all kinds—insects, fishes, amphibians, reptiles, birds, and mammals—have protective coloring. There are insects that look like leaves, twigs, tree bark, berries, and flowers. One side of a flounder looks like the sand on which it usually lies. Quail spend much of their time on the ground, seeking seeds and berries. On their backs are brown, black, and white feathers that have a pattern like the ground and its covering of dead grass and weeds. This protective coloring makes it very hard for flying hawks to see quail on the ground.

A few animals, such as the *chameleon* (a small lizard), can change their coloring to match their surroundings. Some animals that live in snowy regions change the color of their fur or feathers in the winter. The *ptarmigan* (a kind of grouse) and the snowshoe rabbit are white in the winter but dull brown the rest of the year.

For an animal to be protected by its color, the animal should not be moving. A kallima butterfly stand-

Grevy's zebra

ing on a twig looks exactly like a brown, dried leaf. But when the kallima flies, a bird can easily tell that the butterfly is not a dead leaf being blown by the wind.

Very young animals usually cannot move very fast. This makes it hard for them to escape their enemies. Instead of trying to escape, they hide. To hide well, young animals have a special need for protective coloring. Many are born with protective colors. Newly hatched ostriches are the color of the sand on which ostriches live. When danger approaches, baby ostriches "freeze" and remain motionless so that their enemies will not see them. Newly hatched eels are as colorless as the water in which they swim. One kind of protective coloring is called *mimicry*. An animal that cannot defend itself against its enemies, *mimics* (looks like) a similar animal that can defend itself. Hawk moths, which have no stings, mimic bumble bees, which do

◀ Insects often camouflage themselves by taking on the shape and color of a leaf or twig.

have stings. Birds learn not to eat monarch butterflies because they make the birds sick. Birds could safely eat viceroy butterflies. But the viceroy mimics the monarch. So birds do not eat the viceroy, either.

Protective coloring is the result of *natural selection*. A good example of the way natural selection works is shown by a certain kind of moth that lives in Britain. In 1850, most of these moths were light-colored, but some were dark. A hundred years

◀ This African mantis has flaps on its front legs that resemble flower petals. Unwary insects think they are visiting a flower and are grabbed by the mantis.

▲ The bright colors of the South American poison frog warn predators that it should be avoided.

▲ A green tree frog chooses to sit on a green leaf. If it sat on brown bark it would be a more obvious target for predators.

Wasp

Hoverfly

▲ The hoverfly is harmless, but mimics the coloring of a wasp, which can deliver a painful sting. It is therefore avoided by predators.

◀ The stripes on a zebra help to break up the outline of the animal. In long grass it can be almost invisible.

Chameleons can change the color of their skin to match their different surroundings. Their skin has cells which contain colored pigments. Some cells have black pigment, others have red or yellow. A chameleon needs this protective coloring, because it remains in one place for a long time, waiting for prey to come close enough, so it can catapult its sticky tongue and seize its victim.

▲ Proteins are not only found in meat and milk products. Pulses, such as peas and beans, nuts, fish, and eggs, are also good sources of protein.

An adult needs about 2 ounces (60 grams) of protein every day to replace protein lost by wear and tear of the body.

later, in the same region, there were more dark-colored moths than light-colored ones. What had happened? Many factories had been built. Smoke from the factories darkened walls and tree trunks. Birds easily saw the light-colored moths on the darkened walls and trees. But they could not easily see the dark-colored moths. Birds ate more light-colored moths than dark-colored moths. More dark-colored moths lived long enough to lay eggs. So, there came to be more dark-colored moths. The dark color had become a protective coloring.

▶▶▶▶ **FIND OUT MORE** ◀◀◀◀
Animal Defenses; Camouflage; Evolution; Feather; Fur

PROTEIN

Protein is a very important food material. Meat, fish, milk, cheese, cereals, and certain vegetables contain protein. Besides being a food, protein is one of the most important of all the substances that make up plants and animals. Protein is the active part of *protoplasm*, which is the living material of plant and animal cells. Enzymes, some hormones, antigens, and antibodies are proteins. Your body contains thousands of different proteins.

Proteins are huge molecules made up of thousands of atoms. All protein molecules have nitrogen, carbon, hydrogen, and oxygen atoms. In addition, many protein molecules contain sulfur, and some have iodine atoms. Each protein is a chain of chemical building blocks called *amino acids*. There are many kinds of amino acids, but only about 20 are found often in proteins. When amino acids join together, they release a molecule of water and form a bond. Different combinations of amino acids form different kinds of proteins, each with a different structure.

Some of the amino acids necessary for human life must be obtained from food. The exact number depends on a person's age and health. Good protein foods are those that contain all the necessary acids. Meat and cheese are two good protein foods. Gelatin is a poor protein food. It lacks some of the needed amino acids. The digestive juices in your stomach and small intestine break up food proteins into amino acids. These pass through the walls of your intestine and enter your bloodstream. Your blood carries the amino acids to the cells that make up the tissues of your body. The cells link together the amino acids to make new proteins.

▶▶▶▶ **FIND OUT MORE** ◀◀◀◀
Cell; Food; Hormone; Human Body; Nutrition

PROTESTANT CHURCHES

The Protestant churches are branches of Christianity. All of these groups grew out of the Protestant Reformation of the 1500s. These sects broke away from the religious ideas and practices of the Roman Catholic Church. They have many basic beliefs in common, but they differ from each other in certain beliefs and rituals. Throughout the world, there are more than 338 million Protestants.

A branch of Protestantism called Lutheranism was started in the 1500s. Other Protestant groups were formed in England and Switzerland around the same time. Some of the major Protestant denominations today are the Presbyterian, Episcopal, Methodist, Congregational, Baptist, and Lutheran churches. The Disciples of Christ, the United Church of Christ, and the Latter-day Saints (Mormons) also have large memberships. The Society of Friends (Quakers) and Adven-

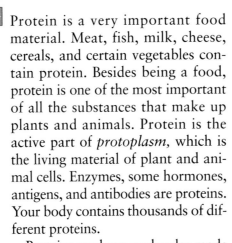

LEADING PROTESTANT GROUPS IN THE UNITED STATES

Group	Membership	Established*	Headquarters
Baptist churches			
American Baptist Churches in the U.S.A.	1,568,778	1907	Valley Forge, Pennsylvania
National Baptist Convention, U.S.A., Inc.	5,500,000	1880	Baton Rouge, Louisiana
National Baptist Convention of America	2,668,799	1880	Little Rock, Arkansas
Southern Baptist Convention	14,722,617	1845	Nashville, Tennessee
Christian Church (Disciples of Christ)	1,086,668	1804	Indianapolis, Indiana
Christian Churches and Churches of Christ	1,071,995	1811	Cincinnati, Ohio
Church of Christ, Scientist (Christian Scientists)	no figure available	1879	Boston, Massachusetts
Church of Jesus Christ of Latter-Day Saints (Mormon)	4,000,000	1830	Salt Lake City, Utah
Church of the Nazarene	543,762	1908	Kansas City, Missouri
Episcopal Church of the U.S.A.	2,462,300	1789	New York, New York
Jehovah's Witnesses	773,219	1884	Brooklyn, New York
Lutheran churches			
American Lutheran Church	2,339,946	1960	Minneapolis, Minnesota
Lutheran Church in America	2,910,281	1962	New York, New York
Lutheran Church-Missouri Synod	2,628,133	1847	St. Louis, Missouri
Methodist churches			
African Methodist Episcopal Church	2,210,000	1816	Washington, D.C.
African Methodist Episcopal Zion Church	1,202,229	1796	Washington, D.C.
Christian Methodist Episcopal Church	466,718	1870	Chicago, Illinois
United Methodist Church	9,291,936	1968	New York, New York
Orthodox Church in America	1,000,000	1792	New York, New York
Pentecostal churches			
Assemblies of God	2,160,667	1914	Springfield, Missouri
Church of God (Cleveland, Tennessee)	505,775	1886	Cleveland, Tennessee
United Pentecostal Church	500,000	1945	Hazlewood, Missouri
Presbyterian churches			
Presbyterian Church in the United States	866,500	1861	Atlanta, Georgia
United Presbyterian Church in the U.S.A.	3,092,151	1958	Philadelphia, Pennsylvania
Salvation Army, The	434,002	1865	New York, New York
Seventh-day Adventists	638,929	1863	Washington, D.C.
United Church of Christ	1,662,568	1957	New York, New York

*Recent dates show that two or more churches have merged.

tists are other Protestant groups.

Most Protestants believe that the Bible is the word of God. They follow its teachings as their religious law, but most of them are free to *interpret* (understand) it as they wish. This is one of the reasons why there are so many different Protestant churches. The groups that believe in accepting every word of the Bible without question are called *fundamentalists.*

Unlike Roman Catholicism, which has a pope, Protestantism does not have a single leader. Protestants often elect officers to serve on regional and national councils of their churches. The head of the national group is called by various names in different denominations, such as bishop, general secretary, or president.

A main idea in Protestantism is the "priesthood of believers." Protestants believe that people can communicate with God through their own faith instead of only through the aid of sacraments given by a priest. Church services are led by a *minister.* Protestant ministers may marry and have families. *Lay people* (members who are not ministers) take part in services and church government. In recent years, women have been ordained as ministers in a number of Protestant churches for the first time.

Much work has been done to try to bring the Protestant churches together. Many U.S. Protestant

▼ **A typical, simple-looking Protestant church in Calais, Vermont.**

In 1976, the Episcopal Church in the United States voted that women might be *ordained* (certified) as priests. Before that, women had always been excluded from the priesthood.

▼ Martin Luther, a German monk, nails a list of 95 theses to the door of the church at Wittenberg in 1517. These were challenges to the authority of the pope.

denominations belong to the National Council of the Churches of Christ. Protestant churches all over the world, including Orthodox Eastern churches, joined in forming the World Council of Churches in 1948. Several individual Protestant churches have joined others in mergers. The United Church of Canada is made up of several churches. Three branches of the Methodist Church joined each other in 1939. The Congregational Christian and the Evangelical and Reformed churches formed the United Church of Christ in 1961. A few traditional Protestant churches have split, and new churches have been formed.

▶▶▶ **FIND OUT MORE** ◀◀◀
Christianity; Jesus Christ; Luther, Martin; Protestant Reformation; Religion; Roman Catholic Church; Society of Friends

PROTESTANT REFORMATION

In Europe in the 1500s, a great religious movement called the Reformation took place. Its aim was to reform, or change, the ways of the Roman Catholic Church. The movement ended with the forming of the Protestant churches.

Early Stirrings of Rebellion
Although the Reformation officially began in 1517, its roots probably go back hundreds of years before that. The Roman Catholic Church was the established church and the most powerful force in Europe. Its popes were even stronger than kings. The popes, kings, and nobles constantly fought with one another over territory. Here and there, people began to question the power of the Catholic popes. One of the first to speak out against the Church was a French merchant, Peter Waldo, in the 1100s. In England, a scholar and priest

named John Wycliffe preached against the Catholic Church from 1368 to 1374. Wycliffe's followers translated the Bible into English. In Bohemia, John Huss was burned at the stake in 1415 for *heresy* (disagreeing with the official beliefs of the Church). The rebirth of learning in the 1400s brought education to more people. Rebellion grew. Many people wanted Christianity to return to its early ways of simple devotion to God. They were angered by the greed and misbehavior of some of the Roman Catholic clergy.

The Reformation Begins
In 1517, a monk named Martin Luther posted 95 *theses* (statements of belief) on a church door in Wittenberg, Germany. In them, he attacked the authority of the pope and many of the practices of the Catholic Church. His followers, the Lutherans, became the first Protestants. Switzerland had two famous Protestant reformers. Ulrich Zwingli led the movement in Zurich in the 1520s. In 1536, in Geneva, John Calvin began to teach Protestant ideas. Calvin had fled from France to escape punishment for his beliefs. He was especially noted for putting Protestant thought into a clear and orderly form. Luther and Calvin are often called the "Fathers of the Reformation."

King Henry VIII of England broke away from the Catholic Church in 1534. Pope Clement VII had refused to *annul* (cancel) the king's first marriage so that he could marry Anne Boleyn. The king announced that from that time on, he, not the pope, would be the head of the Church of England. Henry's daughter, Mary Tudor, as queen, tried to make England Catholic again and burned many Protestant leaders at the stake. Queen Elizabeth I brought Protestantism back to England in 1560. Another Protestant leader was John Knox of Scotland. Knox helped force Mary, Queen of Scots (a Catholic), to give up her throne and leave her country.

Last Years of the Reformation

The Catholic Church did not allow Protestantism to spread without a harsh struggle. It created its own *Counter Reformation*. It called the Council of Trent in 1545 to find a means of stopping the revolution and of bringing self-reform. Despite this, strife between Catholics and Protestants continued. In 1572, Calvin's followers in France, the Huguenots, were murdered by the thousands. A savage religious conflict was fought in Germany and nearby countries from 1618 to 1648. It was called the Thirty Years' War. Over half of the German population died in it.

The Reformation accomplished many of its goals. The Roman Catholic Church no longer ruled without question. Protestant churches were established in many parts of Europe. People began to think of themselves as individuals, with the right to make their own decisions and choose their own beliefs. Out of this newfound freedom of thought came a growth in scholarship, and the scientific achievements of such thinkers as Galileo and Newton. There was an increase in concern with the material world—with life on earth rather than life after death.

▶▶▶▶ **FIND OUT MORE** ◀◀◀◀
Henry, Kings of England;
Luther, Martin; Protestant Churches;
Roman Catholic Church

◀ A scene during the Massacre of St. Bartholomew's Day in 1572, when some 29,000 French Protestants were murdered.

PROTIST

Protists are very small and simple living things. Most plants and animals have many cells and many different kinds of cells. These cells are separated into groups called *tissues*. Each tissue is made up of the same kind of cells. Protists are not divided into tissues. Some protists have only one cell. Other protists have many cells, but all their cells are very much alike.

There are *lower protists* and *higher protists*. The lower protists include bacteria and blue-green algae. The higher protists include all the other algae, protozoa, and fungi.

In 1886, a German biologist, Ernst Haeckel, was the first to suggest using the name "protist" for a group of plants and animals. He suggested it because biologists were having trouble placing fungi and one-celled plants and animals in proper groups in the plant and animal kingdoms. For example, some one-celled living things have cell walls and contain chlorophyll, as plants do. They also move about under their own power, as animals do.

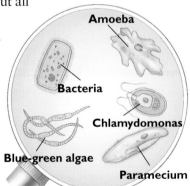

Amoeba

Bacteria

Chlamydomonas

Blue-green algae

Paramecium

▲ The protists include both plants and animals. They are shown here as they appear under a microscope.

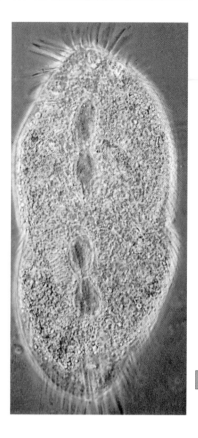

▲ In this microphotograph, a protozoan is shown as it is beginning to narrow in the middle, before it splits into two new cells. The nucleus has already divided.

▼ An amoeba feeds by surrounding a food particle with its flexible body. Here digestive chemicals, from a "bag" called a *vacuole*, dissolve the food.

Are they plants or animals? Haeckel thought that by making a separate group—the protists—he would solve the problem. Haeckel's idea of protists is not accepted by biologists today. They say that the group includes too many unrelated organisms. But the word is still used for one-celled organisms.

▶▶▶▶ **FIND OUT MORE** ◀◀◀◀
Algae; Animal; Cell; Fungus; Plant; Protozoan

PROTOPLASM

SEE CELL

PROTOZOAN

A *protozoan* is an extremely tiny form of animal life. Most protozoa can be seen only under a microscope, but some larger ones grow to be one-quarter or one-half inch (6 to 12 mm) long. There are more than 30,000 different kinds of protozoa, and they live anywhere there is water.

Protozoa by the billions dart through pond and sea water. Others move among the tiny grains of moist soil in a garden. Some are parasites that live inside the bodies of plants and animals. A small puddle of rainwater, left alone for just a few hours, will have a population of protozoa

numbering in the thousands. Protozoa come in many shapes. Some look like round balls, and others are long and thin. They may be shaped like bells or like spirals.

Protozoa are different from other animals in many ways. Protozoa are made of only one cell. Other animals contain many kinds of cells. Some protozoa contain *chlorophyll*, a substance usually found only in plants. Because protozoa are so different from other animals, many scientists think protozoa should not be classified as either plant or animal, but should belong to another special group. This special group is called *protists* or *protista*.

The cell of a protozoan is made up of a lump of living material called *protoplasm*. Inside the protoplasm, a *nucleus* controls the animal's movements and actions. If the nucleus is destroyed, the protozoan dies. Some kinds of protozoa have more than one nucleus, even hundreds of them. Protozoa must have water to live in. Some are so small, however, that a tiny film of water between two grains of desert sand can be enough.

Protozoa get food in several ways. Some absorb dissolved food through the membrane that surrounds their cell of protoplasm. Some protozoa, such as *didiniums*, actually chase and capture their food. Another protozoan, the *amoeba*, can push a part of its body forward to cover and trap its prey. Most protozoa eat tiny particles of living matter. They may feed on bacteria, yeasts, algae, and other protozoa.

Protozoa reproduce by dividing. They split themselves to make two new single-celled animals, each with its own nucleus. Some protozoa produce their offspring on stalks attached to their bodies. A little budlike projection forms and grows. Then the new protozoa split off and start their own lives.

Many protozoa cannot move around under their own power but must depend on the movements of the water. A group of protozoa called

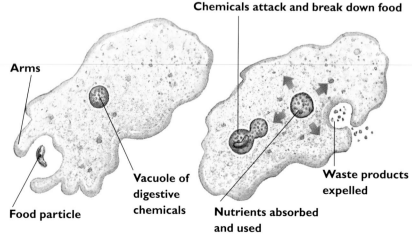

Chemicals attack and break down food

Arms

Food particle

Vacuole of digestive chemicals

Nutrients absorbed and used

Waste products expelled

flagellates are able to move around on their own. They are equipped with a whiplike projection that lashes rapidly back and forth to move the protozoan along. Other protozoa have *cilia*, projections that look like tiny hairs. The cilia move through the water like rows of oars. Still other protozoa (such as the amoeba) creep or flow around by moving the protoplasm in their soft bodies.

The protozoa that normally live in human bodies are harmless, but some kinds of protozoa can cause disease. Malaria is caused by a group of parasitic protozoa called *plasmodia*. One type of amoeba causes a serious disease called *amoebic dysentery*. Sleeping sickness is caused by any of various parasitic protozoa, called *trypanosomes*.

▶▶▶▶ **FIND OUT MORE** ◀◀◀◀
Animal; Animal Kingdom; Cell;
Disease; Parasite; Protist

PSYCHOLOGY AND PSYCHIATRY

Have you ever wondered how your mind works? Where do ideas come from? Why are some people quiet, while others are very talkative? Why do some things make you feel happy, while other things make you sad? What causes you to choose one object or action over other possible choices? These are the kinds of questions that the science of psychology tries to answer. Psychologists study the *minds* and *behavior* of people. Psychiatrists are physicians who, after obtaining an M.D., train to treat and prevent mental illness.

The mind is hard to describe. It is the total of all activities carried on in that part of the brain called the *cerebrum*. Your mind consists of all the ideas, thoughts, feelings, experiences, and memories that you have had, and how you think and feel about them. Your behavior is how you act

as a result of what goes on in the world around you. When you hear something that you think is funny, you laugh. Laughing is a kind of behavior, and so is crying, fighting, humming a tune, tapping a finger, gritting teeth, or sleeping.

Mind and Behavior
Mind and behavior are two important ingredients that make up a person. To learn more about mind and behavior, psychologists study *perception, learning, motivation,* and *personality.*

PERCEPTION. When you see a fire with your eyes, you *perceive* it. Your eyes send a signal to your brain telling you the fire is there. Human beings perceive things through the senses of sight, hearing, touch, taste, and smell. Through these senses, you gather information about the world around you. The mind then sorts out the information so that you can understand it.

LEARNING. When information enters your mind through your senses, the first thing you do is try to understand the information. Small children, for example, may think fire is pretty when they see it. But when they try to touch it, they get burned. In this way, children have learned what fire is like—it's pretty, but also hot! Learning can take place in several ways. Psychologists investigate all the ways of learning to find out which ways work best in various situations. They also study how people use what they have learned in the past in order to learn new things.

MOTIVATION. What makes people do things? Or what makes people want to do things? You have probably heard of police detectives who ask, "What's the *motive* for the crime?" They are asking a psychological question: What is the motivation? Why did the criminal do what he or she did? Let's say you decide to buy an ice-cream cone. You could be motivated to buy it by several things. Perhaps you want something to make

Medical researchers have found that the mind and body are not really independent of each other. If you are physically ill, you probably cannot think in the same way as you do when you are healthy. If you worry too much about something, you can become physically ill.

▲ **Psychologists are concerned with human behavior. Here, a psychologist counsels a young woman who has personal problems.**

A *phobia* is an irrational fear of something. The fear is so strong that it prevents the person from behaving normally. Here are some common and not so common phobias.

Acrophobia fear of heights

Agoraphobia fear of going out of the home or into wide open spaces

Arachnaphobia fear of spiders

Claustrophobia fear of being shut in confined spaces

Hemophobia fear of blood

Hippophobia fear of horses

Microphobia fear of germs

Ophidiophobia fear of snakes

Ornithophobia fear of birds

Phasmophobia fear of ghosts

Triskaidekaphobia fear of the number 13

Xenophobia fear of foreigners

Perhaps the strangest phobia is **phobophobia**, the fear of being afraid.

▼ **How and what a young child draws may reveal to a psychologist how well that child gets along with other young people.**

you feel cool. Maybe someone asked you to buy the ice cream, or maybe you are buying it as a surprise for someone.

Quite often, people do not know or understand why they do certain things. Have you ever felt angry and gotten mad at someone but couldn't explain *why* you got mad? You must have had a reason or motivation, but you didn't know what it was. A boy may buy an ice cream because he thinks he's hungry. But his real motivation may be a wish to make others jealous. Television advertisements are designed to motivate people to do certain things—usually to buy products. Psychologists study people's motivations to find out how they affect behavior and personality.

PERSONALITY. When you say that someone is a grouchy person, a popular person, a shy person, a businesslike person, a funny person, or a nervous person, you are talking about his or her personality. Your personality is that part of your behavior that you show to other people. The words "person" and "personality" come from the Latin word *persona*. In ancient Rome, a persona was the mask that an actor wore on stage.

Your personality is a kind of mask that you wear when you are with other people. Personality is the part of your mind and behavior by which other people know you. There is much of your mind, however, that no one ever knows. It stays deep inside you. When you look at the ocean, you can see the waves and breakers and whatever else is on the surface. But the surface is only one small part of a very big, deep, and often mysterious body of water. Your personality is like the surface of the ocean. It is only a small part of your whole mind.

Branches of Psychology

The science of psychology is divided into several specialties. *Experimental psychologists* do

laboratory research on humans and animals to find out how the senses work and what causes behavior. The *psychology of learning* studies how people learn—how they get ideas and how they put ideas to use. One field of learning psychology is *educational psychology* that studies the problems of learning in schools. *Child psychologists* study the growth and development of babies and young people.

The *psychology of individual differences* tries to discover why people act alike or differently from each other. Psychologists in this field have created many kinds of tests to determine a person's individual characteristics. For example, some tests measure your interests—what you like or don't like to do. Some are intelligence tests that measure how well you can learn certain things, as compared with everyone else of your age or background. Some tests measure aptitudes—the things that you have a talent for or are likely to do well in. Other tests measure personality, achievement (what you have learned so far), and attitudes (your opinions about things). These tests are used by many people—teachers, counselors, and job interviewers—to determine who you are and what your strengths and weaknesses may be.

Abnormal psychology is the study of mental or emotional problems. Psychologists and psychiatrists try to find out the causes of these problems and suggest ways of working them out. They use several methods of treatment, but the main kinds are *somatic therapy* and *psychotherapy*. Somatic therapy involves the use of various drugs. Psychiatrists—not psychologists—can prescribe drugs. Psychotherapy is based on discussions between the patient and psychologist or psychiatrist.

Social psychologists study the behavior of people in groups. They are interested in how groups of people treat each other in different situations, and they study how one group behaves toward another group. For example, a social psychologist would be interested in studying how a group of sixth graders behaves toward a group of third or fourth graders. *Personnel* and *industrial psychologists* deal with people at their jobs. Industrial psychologists use tests to find out what kind of job a person is suited for. They also help workers who are having trouble doing their work.

History of Psychology

Psychology became established as a science in 1879, when Wilhelm Wundt set up the first psychological laboratory in Leipzig, Germany. Between that time and the 1930s, four different ways of studying the mind were developed. These approaches or methods are called *structuralism, behaviorism, gestalt psychology,* and *psychoanalysis.*

The structural psychologists tried to describe and analyze the way people experience or perceive things through their senses. For example, the sense of sight gives the mind a great deal of information, such as shape, color, distance, size, and so on. The sense of touch gives information about texture, heat, cold, pain, wetness, and so on. The structural psychologists wanted to find out what kinds of information the human mind was receiving.

The behavioral psychologists began laboratory experiments on the way people and animals behave in various situations. The Russian scientist Ivan Pavlov had conducted experiments on the reflexes of dogs. Behavioral psychologists extended those experiments to find out how people or animals *usually* behave, *if* behavior can be changed, and *how* behavior can be changed.

The gestalt psychologists were interested in how people's minds are organized—how the mind sorts out information. Gestalt is a German word meaning "pattern" or "form." Gestalt psychologists believed that people perceive things in patterns or groups. For example, when you look at a tree, you perceive a whole object that has a trunk, branches, leaves, roots, and so on. You do not first see leaves, then a trunk, then branches, each separately. Gestalt psychologists created tests to determine the patterns of perception that people have. The most famous of these is the inkblot test, in which a person describes the shapes and objects that he thinks he sees in the inkblot.

Psychoanalysis began around 1900, with the work of Dr. Sigmund Freud. Freud believed that persons tend to *repress* (push out of their conscious, or thinking, mind) any thoughts or memories that they or other people do not approve of. Freud said that these repressed thoughts and memories have a great effect on people's behavior. Through psychoanalysis, people could be made to remember their repressed thoughts and memories, and then be able to change their behavior and work out their mental problems.

▶▶▶▶ **FIND OUT MORE** ◀◀◀◀
Branches of Psychology,
see Aging; Extra Sensory Perception; Growth; Intelligence; Learning; Mental Health
Elements in the Study of Psychology see Adolescence; Brain; Culture; Customs; Dream; Emotion; Habit; Health; Hormone; Human Body; Hypnosis; Memory; Nervous System; Reasoning; Sense Organ
Psychologists see Freud, Sigmund; Jung, Carl; Pavlov, Ivan
Science and Other Related Fields to Psychology see Anthropology; Child Care; Education; Genetics; Guidance; Medicine; Philosophy; Science; Social Work; Sociology; Special Education; Teaching

▲ **Psychologists use tests to find out about people. Test your short-term memory by looking at these objects for 30 seconds. Cover them up and see how many you can remember.**

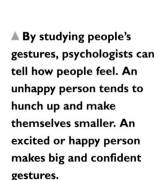

▲ **By studying people's gestures, psychologists can tell how people feel. An unhappy person tends to hunch up and make themselves smaller. An excited or happy person makes big and confident gestures.**

In the 1700s in England, even the rich rarely washed their whole body. Face and hands were washed in soap and water each morning. The rest of the body was occasionally rubbed down with a cloth soaked in rose water.

PUBERTY

SEE ADOLESCENCE

PUBLIC HEALTH

You and your schoolmates receive vaccinations to keep you from getting diseases that can be spread from one person to another. You drink water without any fear that it will give you a disease. Providing health education and making water safe to drink are public health actions. *Public health* is the field of medicine and hygiene that deals with preventing diseases in the community.

Almost every community has a department of public health. This department is responsible for a number of things. It enforces standards of cleanliness for the handling and preparing of foods in restaurants. It makes sure that garbage taken away from homes and streets so that these wastes are not a threat to the health of the people. It gives advice to women on how to care for their health before their babies are born, and then advises them on how to care for their babies and small children.

The public health department keeps records on what diseases the citizens suffer. It sets standards for the construction and care of public vehicles (buses, trains, and so on), recreation centers, beaches, and private, as well as public, buildings. The public health department made sure that when your school was built it had enough windows, good plumbing, and an adequate system for getting rid of garbage. In larger communities, public health departments have nurses who, among their other duties, visit and help old and feeble persons in their homes.

People who work in public health must have medical and scientific training. Public health workers include doctors, nurses, and those trained for special jobs, such as testing the purity of water.

The idea of public health was understood in a small way even in ancient times. Cities had laws that required garbage and other wastes to be kept out of certain parts of a city. People had some idea that there was a connection between filth and disease. In the 1800s, bacteria and viruses were discovered to be the causes of diseases that can be passed from one person to another. Once this was understood, laws governing public health were passed to help prevent the spread of diseases.

The Public Health Service is an agency of the Department of Health and Human Services. The Public Health Service is directed by the surgeon general. One of its bureaus enforces quarantine laws to prevent epidemics and examines immigrants to make sure they do not have

▶ The Food Guide Pyramid is published by the U.S. Department of Agriculture, and supported by the Department of Health and Human Services. This is just one of the ways that public health services help to improve the health of the nation.

Food Guide Pyramid

A Guide to Daily Food Choices

Fats, Oils, & Sweets
USE SPARINGLY

KEY
☐ Fat (naturally occurring and added)   ◻ Sugars (added)

These symbols show fat and added sugars in foods.

Milk, Yogurt, & Cheese Group
2-3 SERVINGS

Meat, Poultry, Fish, Dry Beans, Eggs, & Nuts Group
2-3 SERVINGS

Vegetable Group
3-5 SERVINGS

Fruit Group
2-4 SERVINGS

Bread, Cereal, Rice, & Pasta Group
6-11 SERVINGS

Use the Food Guide Pyramid to help you eat better every day. ...the Dietary Guidelines way. Start with plenty of Breads, Cereals, Rice, and Pasta; Vegetables; and Fruits. Add two to three servings from the Milk group and two to three servings from the Meat group. Each of these food groups provides some, but not all, of the nutrients you need. No one food group is more important than another — for good health you need them all. Go easy on fats, oils, and sweets, the foods in the small tip of the Pyramid.

LEARN BY DOING

You can do much to contribute to public health. Stay away from others as much as you can when you have a cold or any other illness that is contagious. Cover your nose and mouth when you cough or sneeze. Keep all garbage and waste in closed containers. If you pass an uncovered garbage can on the street, cover it! Don't drink water if you are not sure it is pure. Report anything that you think is a menace to public health.

diseases others can catch. It also operates federal hospitals and clinics. Another bureau helps states, foreign governments, and organizations operate health programs. The National Institutes of Health study physical and mental diseases.

▶▶▶▶ **FIND OUT MORE** ◀◀◀◀
Bacteria; Contagious Diseases;
Immunity; Virus

PUBLIC RELATIONS

The art of winning people's favor for an organization or an individual is known as public relations. Many businesses (car makers, airlines, hotels, and so on) employ experts in public relations to inform the public and get them to think positively about the organization.

To do this, public relations people try to have favorable stories about their employers published in newspapers, magazines, or books. They try to use radio and television programs for the same purpose. They give free photographs of the people or places they are publicizing to newspapers and magazines. Sometimes they entertain important customers who visit the company.

Public relations and advertising are closely connected. Public relations helps to "sell" a company to the public. Advertising helps to sell the goods that company produces. Sometimes public relations and advertising work together to promote both the company and its products. For example, a sporting goods store might buy baseball shirts for a Little League team. By doing this, the store manager may hope to get good publicity for the store and also sell products to league members and others in the community.

People who use public relations firms include men and women who are candidates for election to public office. The public relations experts

try to build what they call a favorable image of their client. They want to make the voters like the candidate so much that they will vote for him or her.

▶▶▶▶ **FIND OUT MORE** ◀◀◀◀
Public Speaking

PUBLIC SPEAKING

If you have ever made a speech to your class, you already know something about public speaking. You determined that you must know your subject well in order to earn the respect of your audience.

You know that your speech must be interesting to make your audience listen to you at all. Experienced speakers are also aware that they must understand their audience's interests and opinions.

A speech should be well organized. In the *introduction*, the speaker should attract the listeners' attention and make them want to hear the speech. In the *body* of the speech, the speaker should state the main ideas and explain them clearly. The kind of explanation depends on the requirements of the speech. Examples, facts, reasons, and comparisons are frequently used to support the main ideas. The *conclusion* should present a brief summary of what the speaker has said. The conclusion helps the audience remember the most important points of the speech.

Like all other kinds of communication, public speaking involves a message to send, a sender, and a

▲ Queen Elizabeth II of Britain has little real power, but she does an important public relations job for her country, at home and abroad.

▼ Your first experience of public speaking will probably take place at a school gathering.

► In 1933, the U.S. government set up the Tennessee Valley Authority (TVA) to control floods, improve navigation, and produce electricity in the region of the Tennessee River and its tributaries. The Norris dam, shown here, was the first dam to be built by the TVA, a public utility company.

There are many long speeches on record in the United States Senate. The longest continuous speech was delivered by Senator Wayne Morse in 1953. He spoke for 22 hours, 26 minutes without sitting down!

TOP PUBLIC UTILITIES ON THE NEW YORK STOCK EXCHANGE

American Electric Power
Centerior Energy
Commonwealth Edison
Consolidated Edison
Consolidated Natural Gas
Detroit Edison
Houston Industries
Niagara Mohawk Power
Pacific Gas & Electric
Panhandle Eastern
Peoples Energy
Philadelphia Electric
Public Service Enterprises
SCE

receiver. In this case, there is a spoken message (the speech), a speaker, and listeners. Each plays an equally important part.

The public speaker stirs up ideas and feelings in the listeners in many ways. What the audience sees influences its opinion of the speaker and his or her message. The speaker's posture, gestures, facial expression, and body movements are all important. The way the speaker uses his or her voice can change the meaning of the speech. The loudness of sounds, their pitch (high, medium, and low), and the emphasis put on words influence the meaning of what is said. Some words have several possible meanings, and the listener can tell which meaning is intended by the speaker's voice. The choice of words also affects the way the listener will react.

Most public speeches are one of three general kinds. The speech meant to *inform* is intended to give the audience information on a particular subject. For example, if you gave a speech to your class on caring for a pet rabbit, the speech would be informative. A speech intended to *persuade* tries to convince the audience that the speaker's opinions are correct. Speeches given by politicians are persuasive speeches. The speech meant to *entertain* is amusing (if it is successful), and helps create a mood of easy enjoyment. For example, speeches given at banquets are often meant simply to entertain.

▶▶▶▶ **FIND OUT MORE** ◀◀◀◀
Pronunciation; Speech

PUBLIC UTILITY

When you turn on a lamp in your house, you are using a public utility. Public utilities are businesses that supply services such as light, heat, power, telephone, telegraph, water, and garbage disposal. Transportation services are also public utilities. These include delivery services, airplanes, buses, subways, and trains.

Public utilities are owned by the government in many countries. But in the United States, most public utilities are owned by private companies. The federal government, however, does carefully regulate the way in which some public utilities are run. The government tells public utility companies how much to charge for their services.

Some cities and towns own public utilities. Local city or town governments sometimes own airports, bus and subway systems, water supply systems, garbage disposal facilities, and sewage systems.

The federal government owns some of the power plants that supply electricity in the United States. The Tennessee Valley Authority is the best known of these U.S. government-owned public utilities.

A public utility company is usually the only one in an area to provide a certain service. This means that the company has a *monopoly* on the service. Because public utility companies provide important services, communities depend on them. A strike at a public utility—so that garbage is not picked up or telephones don't work—can cause a community crisis. Government regulation of public utilities is therefore necessary.

▶▶▶▶ **FIND OUT MORE** ◀◀◀◀
Electric Power;
Telecommunications; Telegraph;
Telephone; Tennessee; Transportation;
Water Supply

PUBLISHING

The business of selecting, editing, printing, advertising, and distributing printed material is called *publishing*. Publishing companies put written words and *visuals* (pictures, photographs, charts, and diagrams) together to produce books, magazines, newspapers, pamphlets, and other types of printed material.

Although publishing techniques differ depending on the material being published, the general process is similar for all types of material. Let's say you have written a book, and you want to have it published. First you send a typed copy of your book (called the *manuscript)* to a publishing company. Several *editors* decide whether or not to publish it.

If your book is accepted for publication, an editor works with you in *revising* (changing) or rewriting the manuscript, if necessary. Then a *copy editor* prepares it for the printer. The copy editor corrects any mistakes in grammar, spelling, or punctuation, and checks to be sure all information in the manuscript is correct.

The editor and a *designer* work together to decide your book's *layout*. They determine the size of the page, the number of pages, and the design of the book's cover (called the *binding*) and the book jacket, if there is to be one.

Once the layout is established, the *production* department goes to work. Your manuscript is marked with directions to the printer on how to set it in type. The typesetter does a sample setting that comes back to the editor on long sheets of paper called *galleys*. *Proofreaders* check the galleys word for word against your original manuscript to be sure the material has been set in type correctly. An extra set of galleys is cut apart and pasted onto rough layouts of the book, with space left for the visuals. These rough layouts become a *working dummy*.

The corrected galleys and the dummy are returned to the printer to be set in final page form, according to the arrangement in the dummy. *Page proofs* follow, and finally come proofs with visuals in place in order to allow a last check. Then a certain number of copies of your book are printed, bound, and shipped to places where they will be sold.

The first book in English published in the United States was the *Bay Psalm Book*. It was printed by Stephen Day in 1640, in Cambridge, Massachusetts.

▼ Using a desktop publishing system, an editor can make up the pages of a book, newspaper, or magazine. The pages can then either become an "electronic" book on disk, or be printed.

Some publishers now use sophisticated computers to lay out and typeset material. This is called desktop publishing (D.T.P.). It cuts out some

▲ **A designer at work in a publishing house.**

of the stages, making the publishing process quicker and cheaper.

Long before the final printing, plans are made for selling your book. The sales and marketing departments decide how many copies will be printed and where and how they will be sold. Promotion schemes (publicity and advertising) are put into action to arouse people's interest in your book. Finally, salespeople sell your book to bookstores, which sell it to their customers.

Many types of publishing companies produce different kinds of material. There are two types of *book publishers. Trade book publishers*

handle all books of general interest to the public, such as fiction, poetry, history, biographies, cooking, reference books, and many others. *Educational publishers* handle textbooks, workbooks, and any other printed materials written to instruct students and intended to be sold to schools. Some publishers handle both trade and educational books.

Magazine publishing is divided into general-interest *mass magazines* and *special-interest magazines* (such as scientific hobby magazines, and so on). *Newspaper publishing* involves the production of printed news. Newspapers are divided into categories according to the size of readership and frequency of circulation (whether they are published daily, weekly, or monthly).

►►►► FIND OUT MORE ◄◄◄◄

Advertising; Book; Communication; Design; Journalism; Magazine; Newspaper; Photography; Printing; Typesetting

---

LEARN BY DOING

If you should become interested in working in the publishing industry, there is a wide variety of jobs available in writing, editing, proofreading, photography, art, design, typesetting, printing, advertising, marketing, selling, and many others. You can begin right now to get experience, by working on a school newspaper or magazine. If your school does not have one, why not start one!

QUIZ ANSWERS

Photography quiz, page 2066
1. Most 35mm cameras use either cassette or roll film.
2. 200 ASA film is faster (good in most light levels and for catching subjects that are moving fast).
3. A film's negative is a "reversed-out" version of an image. On the negative, white (or lighter) areas show up as dark areas, while black (dark) areas show up as light areas. Light is then directed through the negative onto specially treated paper to make the positive image—the photographic print.
4. Color-negative film (which produces color prints) and color film that produces slides are the two types of color film.
5. George Eastman in 1888 designed a simple camera that was light and easy to use.

Plant quiz, page 2089
1. The cell walls of a plant are made of cellulose.
2. Xylem are the tubes that carry water upward in a plant's stem.
3. The four groups in the plant kingdom are made up of (1) the simplest plants (such as lichens), (2) the slightly more complex (such as mosses), (3) plants with leaves and roots but no seeds (such as ferns), and (4) seed plants (such as flowers and pine trees).
4. Tropism is the movement of a plant in response to something outside of it, such as sunshine.
5. Sweet potatoes and carrots (and also radishes and beets) are actually roots.

Plastic quiz, page 2102
1. In 1869, John W. Hyatt invented celluloid, the first plastic.
2. The two main plastics are thermoplastic and thermosetting.
3. Acrylic (thermoplastic) and epoxy (thermosetting) are both used to make paint. Polyesters (thermosetting) are used to make boats.
4. Plastic can be shaped either by molding it, casting it, extruding it, calendering it, or laminating it.
5. Phonograph records, raincoats, garden hoses, and upholstery are a few of the objects that can be made of vinyl.

Presidency quiz, page 2150
1. The President is in charge of the executive branch.
2. There are 14 executive departments under the President.
3. Theodore Roosevelt was 42 when he became President. John F. Kennedy was only slightly older, at 43.
4. Franklin Delano Roosevelt was elected to four consecutive terms (1933–1945). He died during his fourth term. William Henry Harrison (1773–1841) caught pneumonia during the inauguration ceremony and died soon after. He was President for 31 days.
5. Fourteen vice presidents went on to become President: John Adams, Thomas Jefferson, Martin Van Buren, *John Tyler, Millard Fillmore, Andrew Johnson, Chester A. Arthur, Theodore Roosevelt, Calvin Coolidge, Harry Truman,* Richard Nixon, *Lyndon Johnson,* Gerald Ford, and George Bush. (The eight names in italics took office when the elected president died or was killed in office.)